Weekend Haunts

A guide to haunted hotels in the UK

Robin Mead

i
impact books

Acknowledgements

This book could not have been written without the advice, assistance and information provided by various organisations and companies. They include the British Tourist Authority, whose former deputy chief executive Alan Jefferson suggested the original idea; the Scottish Tourist Board; the various English regional tourist boards; the British Hospitality Association, and especially its secretary Peter Catchpole; Consort Hotels; and Forte Hotels.

The author would also like to thank the following individuals for their help and ideas – much of it provided above and beyond the call of duty: Jackey Allen, Priscilla Chapman, Wally Croft, Margaret Fotheringham, Andrew Franklin, Stuart Harrison, Gillian Harrower, Eddie Holmes, Matthew Hutton, Zoe McAndry, Meta Maltman, Bob Meredith, Susan Nicholls, Gillian Pope, Malcolm Powell, Geoff Thomas, Christine Travell and Mike Weaver.

Special thanks go to Pamela Wright, for her wonderful drawings, and to Felicity Sinclair, who typed the manuscript. But, above all, the author owes a debt of gratitude to his partner, Polly, who did all the research, kept everything on schedule – and even met a couple of quite credible ghosts.

First published in Great Britain 1994
by Impact Books Ltd, 151 Dulwich Road, London SE24 0NG

© Robin Mead 1994

All rights reserved. No part of this publication may be reproduced in any form or by any means whatsoever without the prior consent of Impact Books Ltd.

All information and advice included in this book is given in good faith, and every effort has been made to ensure that the details are correct at time of pubication. Nevertheless, neither the author nor the publishers can accept any responsibility of whatsoever nature for any errors or omissions, inaccuracy of information or advice, or for any changes in details given.

ISBN: 1 874687 34 X

Designed and typeset by Paperweight Print Production and Design Consultants, London SE24

Printed and bound by the Guernsey Press, Guernsey

Contents

Acknowledgements ii

Introduction iv

A–Z of Hotels **1**

Regional Maps 162

Alphabetical Index 181

Regional Index 184

Introduction

Let's get one thing clear from the start: this is not a book for, or from, the lunatic fringe. It is, first and foremost, a hotel guide book – and on its pages you will find described, in some detail, a selection of the best hotels in Britain.

The hotels vary immensely in size, and price. They include some of the grandest establishments in the country. But they also include some very small properties and even a bed-and-breakfast establishment or two. And they all have two things in common.

Firstly, they offer good value for money and, as the title of this book suggests, they are all very nice places at which to take a weekend break, or perhaps spend a longer holiday. Secondly, as the title again suggests, visitors to these hotels may find that not all of their fellow guests are necessarily of the tangible variety.

Britain has well over 350 haunted hotels, and these are a selection of those properties. Overseas visitors to Britain tend to think that ghosts are a uniquely British phenomenon – a phenomenon perhaps based on the twilight world of Celtic folklore. Certainly, the Celtic parts of the British Isles have their share of ghosts, along with rather more than their fair share of legends, superstitions, and general creepiness.

What could be creepier than Dartmoor, on a misty autumn night? Or some of the lonelier Scottish islands, locked in their sea-girt fastness? Well, some old-established settlements in New England might answer: 'Us'. There's a worldwide population of ghosts, their habitat ranging from Australia's aboriginal lands to the snowy summits of Tibet, and from the plains where the North American Indians once roamed to the isolated villages of Crete.

But Britain's ghosts, unseen though they usually are, are a tourist attraction in their own right. No self-respecting castle is without its ghost. Hundreds of pubs claim them. Indeed, my 'local' has an elderly gent who occupies his favourite seat by the window and enjoys a pint but who, on closer examination, is not really there. No, I haven't seen him myself – but it makes a nice story on winter evenings.

And, of course, the thousands of large country houses scattered across the length and breadth of Britain, and built in a more prosperous age, are full of ghosts. Many of those old country houses have now been converted into luxurious country house hotels. They come complete with open views, open fireplaces and, more often than not, a spooky story or two from their past. Central heating, let alone the care lavished on them by their new owners, means that their atmosphere nowadays tends towards the homely rather than the hair-raising. But the first question that many overseas guests ask when they arrive at such places is, more often than not: 'Have you got a ghost?'.

In these pages you will find a selection of those which can answer: 'Yes'. And the stories which the hoteliers have to tell are extraordinarily varied. Some are sad, some are puzzling, and one or two are even funny. The spirit world, it seems, is not without its sense of humour.

But I don't think that any of the ghosts which may, or may not, inhabit the hotels in this book are frightening. There are no screaming banshees or chain-rattling ghouls to disturb your slumbers. Nevertheless some haunted hotels, fearful that a ghost story might put off some prospective customers, have asked not to be included – and I have respected their wishes.

Other properties make a positive feature of their ghost. Up in Scotland, for example, owner Tony Ptolomey takes visitors on a candlelit tour of the spookier parts of his hotel at Comlongon Castle before dinner – and I can vouch for the fact that it is a nerve-tingling experience. A couple of other well-known English hotels actively encourage ghost-hunts of an evening – but that may be because their ghosts are handily housed in rooms now doing duty as the bar.

Most of the hotels in this book, however, treat their resident ghost as they would treat any other long-term resident: with a sort of cheery familiarity tempered with a modicum of respect.

Until its demise due to government financial cutbacks, I was the only lay member of the British Tourist Authority's hotel commendation scheme's judging panel. This panel, under the chairmanship of the redoubtable Countess Spencer, was responsible for ensuring that hotels both large and small achieved, and maintained, a degree of comfort and service that cannot be reflected in any number of stars, crowns, or whatever other symbols the travel industry adopts to classify hotels. All of the hotels in this book have been personally inspected, and I like to think that they would meet the high standards demanded by the commendation panel and that they would survive even the former Lady Spencer's eagle eye.

So, if you don't see or hear a ghost, you will at least have a nice holiday. But if you experience something out of the ordinary, or if you know of a haunted hotel, then I would love to know.

Perhaps you will even succeed where I failed, and find a haunted hotel in central London. But you will have to hurry, because as I write the old St George's Hospital, overlooking Hyde Park Corner, has become the very up-market Lanesborough Hotel. And two quite differing sources say that, while it was a hospital, the building contained the ghost of a nineteenth-century nurse who was frequently seen by staff gliding down the stairs. One of the people who told me this story is a former matron at the hospital – and you don't argue with matron!

Happy ghost-hunting!

Robin Mead

01 ALVESTON MANOR   Heart of England

Clopton Bridge, Stratford-upon-Avon, Warwickshire CV37 7HP
Telephone: 0789-204581
Fax: 0789-414095

> *Rooms:* include 18 double, 77 twin
> *Location:* Central but peaceful   *Price Range:* £££
> *Restaurant:* à la carte ££; table d'hôte £
> *Facilities:* Historic building; extensive grounds

Once a upon a time, as Shakespeare would not have put it, a Norman manor house stood in acres of farmland just outside a little Warwickshire village that was later to attain fame as the birthplace of the bard: Stratford-upon-Avon. Today that manor house is the lovely Alveston Manor hotel.

Built in Tudor times, in glowing red brick and with exposed timbers, the building is an impressive sight. In Shakespeare's day, it is said, the author staged the first performance of *A Midsummer Night's Dream* in its garden, using a vast cedar tree as backdrop. That tree is still there.

Inside the hotel there is a multitude of ancient beams and carved doors, often with massive bosses and iron hinges still in perfect condition. The comfortable lounges have fine panelling and the fireplaces are huge – with stone or tile surrounds framing the flames. Antiques and old prints are everywhere.

The restaurant serves delightful meals based on traditional English cooking, spiced with elegant international dishes. The surroundings are cosy, with the images of England's kings and queens beaming down on diners from the stained glass windows.

The hotel has 110 bedrooms. There are some particularly elegant rooms in the old part of the hotel, with arched ceilings, historic four-poster beds and antique furniture. Other rooms are in the new part of the building and are very comfortably furnished in a timeless period style. All the rooms are spacious, and gracious, and have every modern amenity.

The village of Stratford-upon-Avon is a pretty, if slightly over-commercialised, place – but the original buildings that house the bard's birthplace and the home of his wife, Anne Hathaway, are essential stopping places for Shakespeare lovers. The Royal Shakespeare Theatre stages performances every day in season, at the Memorial Theatre, and the river Avon is a delight for boating or for walking. The historic town of Warwick with its castle, and Coventry with its modern cathedral, are nearby.

THE GHOST is that of a monk, who apparently stayed on after links between the one-time manor house and a nearby monastery were broken.

A tunnel linked house and monastery – and traffic along it was two way. The family who owned the manor house used it to go and worship in the monastery chapel, while the monks used it to pay both official and unofficial visits to the cellar full of fine wines.

All that was 500 years ago, but one monk has been happy to make his visit an extended one. He is often heard carousing in the cellars: staff report hearing the sound of clinking glasses, slurping noises, and ancient but far-from-religious bursts of song. But, when they investigate, the cellars are empty.

02 AMBERLEY CASTLE South East England

Amberley, nr Arundel, West Sussex BN18 9ND
Telephone: 0798-831992
Fax: 0798-831998

Amberley Castle

Rooms: 11 double, 1 twin
Location: Rural   *Price Range:* £££
Restaurant: The Queen's Room (à la carte £££; table d'hôte ££)
Facilities: Historic building

Until very recently, you would have had no chance of enjoying the comforts of Amberley Castle unless you were a bishop or visiting nobility. Because it was a Bishop's Palace, and later a private home, the castle – nestling behind its superb medieval curtain wall – remained hidden from prying eyes for more than 900 years.

But in 1988, hoteliers Martin and Joy Cummings took the plunge and turned this beautiful building into one of England's most elegant and atmospheric hotels.

They have taken the castle buildings, set around an inner courtyard, and lovingly restored them without losing any of the flavour that Queen Elizabeth I knew and enjoyed when she stayed at Amberley Castle in the latter years of her reign. The entrance is still through the massive and imposing gatehouse, complete with portcullis and oubliette. But behind the gatehouse and the curtain wall, the visitor enters a tranquil grassy courtyard with rooms on one side and terraced shrubberies on the other. The oak-doored main castle building, which contains the public rooms and some of the bedrooms, beckons invitingly.

Inside, great open fireplaces house roaring log fires in season. Suits of armour, tapestries, oil paintings and antiques enliven the panelling, and there are rich rugs on the stone flags. They say that every man's home is his castle, but in this case the Cummings' castle could not be more homely.

A discerning tenant in the reign of King Charles II adapted the high-ceilinged banqueting hall into two levels. The upper storey is now the charming Queen's Room restaurant. Guests dine in elegant and historic surroundings, beneath the ornate barrel-vaulted ceiling and a beautiful fresco, painted in 1686, which shows Charles II and his Queen, Catherine of Braganza, out hunting. The excellent meals are served at a leisurely pace, but the choice is sometimes limited and portions may seem small.

The ground-floor portion has now become a library and cosy lounges, where drinks and canapes are served before dinner.

None of the hotel's 12 luxurious bedrooms are the same. Those not in the main building are in an adjoining one, and each has been furnished to an individual scheme by Joy Cummings, following themes suggested by the room's name and setting. Some have four-poster beds. All have every imaginable luxury, including whirlpool bath, direct-dial telephone, TV, video – and a library of video films.

Amberley Castle, surrounded by the watermeadows of the peaceful River Arun, is a splendid base for touring the Sussex downlands and coast. Nearby attractions include Arundel (for its castle and antique shops), Chichester (cathedral and theatre), and Brighton (beaches, sports facilities, shopping).

THE GHOST is that of a young girl, Emily, who haunts the old kitchen area. A figure is sometimes seen there, and she is often heard moaning.

The haunting dates from the fourteenth century, when Emily, a serving girl who worked in the old kitchens, was seduced by one of the medieval bishops – possibly Bishop Rede – who lived there when the castle was owned by the church. It was Bishop Rede, incidentally, who built the curtain wall which is the castle's outstanding architectural attraction and which was intended to protect the wealthy ecclesiastical inhabitants from the attentions of pirates who at that time sailed up and down the River Arun.

Emily died after her seduction – although it is not known whether the cause was remorse, childbirth, or something more mundane such as malaria (then a hazard due to the Amberley Wildbrooks marshland below the castle). Restoration workers and present staff have reported hearing, and very occasionally seeing, Emily at or near the site of the old kitchens, which were just outside the castle wall on the north side. The owners, Martin and Joy Cummings, have never seen or heard anything, and there are no reports of the hotel's guests ever crossing Emily's path. The visitor's closest acquaintance with her is therefore likely to be in the Queen's Room restaurant – where the chef has sentimentally named a pudding after her.

03 THE ANGEL & ROYAL HOTEL

East Midlands

High Street, Grantham, Lincolnshire NG31 6PN
Telephone: 0476-65816
Fax: 0476-67149

Rooms: include 13 double, 6 twin
Location: Central   *Price Range:* £££
Restaurant: à la carte ££; table d'hôte £
Facilities: Historic building

Inns don't come much older or more historic than the Angel & Royal. Built some 800 years ago as a hostel for the crusading brotherhood of the Knights Templar, it was purloined by King John in 1213 as a base for his court. Once he had faded from the scene, the lavish building constructed in mellow stone became an inn for nobles on their travels.

King Edward III's emblem – an angel carrying a crown – is over the doorway and commemorates his visit in the early fifteenth century. The reception area has a Georgian fireplace. In 1483, King Richard III had the bad news of the Duke of Buckingham's treachery – which led to Richard's ultimate defeat at the battle of Bosworth Field – brought to him in the inn's 'Chambre du Roi', which is now the restaurant. Today the room still looks much as it must have done then: it has stone walls draped with tapestries and serves a suitably English menu. The adjacent bar has the air of a medieval hall, and even the seats are tapestry.

The Angel & Royal's 30 bedrooms are all pleasantly furnished in a modern international style, and besides the usual amenities some have trouser presses and mini-bars. Perhaps surprisingly for such a historic building, there are no four-poster beds – but antique accessories do give the bedrooms a period touch.

Uniquely, there is an indoor curling rink at the hotel – very popular with guests who have never tried this sport before. Other, more commonplace, sports are found within easy reach.

Grantham is a pretty town, and has many stately homes in its immediate area, including Belton House and Grantham House, built in the fourteenth century. The church of St Wulfram, in the town, has a rare library of sixteenth-century books: chained then, as now, against light-fingered browsers. Within easy reach are the medieval cities of Lincoln and Nottingham, and the flat reclaimed lands of the Fens with their wildlife and horticulture.

THE GHOST is that of an unknown woman, wearing white, who paces the corridors of the second and third floors of the Georgian part of the hotel. She is seen quite frequently by both staff and guests.

Some guests may also enjoy – if that is the word – a closer acquaintance with the lady in white, for she occasionally gives the bed in one of the guest rooms a vigorous shaking.

Which room? The hotel management aren't saying, because they don't want any squeamish customers put off. But if it should happen to you, don't worry: the experience is described as being a bit like clambering on to a water bed and the white lady, having given visitors a rude awakening, at least has the courtesy to let them spend the rest of the night in peace.

04 ATHOLL PALACE — Tayside & Grampian

Pitlochry, Perthshire PH16 5LY, Scotland
Telephone: 0796-2400
Fax: 0796-3036

> *Rooms:* include 29 double, 35 twin, 9 family rooms
> *Location:* Rural   *Price Range:* £££
> *Restaurant:* à la carte ££; table d'hôte £
> *Facilities:* Lift; swimming pool; tennis; pitch-and-putt; extensive grounds

A Scottish baronial castle, all turrets and flying flags, has been turned into the magnificent Atholl Palace Hotel. Set in woodlands, beside the River Tummel, this hotel offers the best of Scottish hospitality – as it has done since Victorian times. It is a vast building, hiding many lounges and meeting rooms behind its granite walls.

To walk into the Atholl Palace is to enter a world of Victorian opulence; corridors are wide, rooms are high, and the chandeliers glitter. The lounges, with their panoramic views over the hills, are extremely comfortable and furnished in period style with log fires. The Verandah Restaurant is a bright and pretty place to dine, with fine views. The menu offers a range of Scottish specialities alongside a selection of international favourites, and local beef and game feature strongly.

The Atholl Palace's 84 bedrooms are all spacious and very comfortable. Decorated in a range of styles and colour schemes to suit each room's ambience, they all have modern conveniences. But period furniture and old paintings and prints on the walls add plenty of atmosphere.

The hotel is almost a resort in its own right. The pleasant grounds include a swimming pool, tennis courts, and a pitch-and-putt course. And, if you've a mind, you can even arrive by helicopter, landing on the hotel's own helipad.

The town of Pitlochry has more sports to offer – golf and salmon or trout fishing in particular. It stages a famous international arts festival each summer, from May to October. Nearby is Blair Castle, well worth a visit, and if the Highland air gives you a thirst you could visit the smallest distillery in Scotland, the Edradour Distillery, just a short drive away. Dundee, with its maritime heritage and Scott of the Antartic's ship *Discovery*, is a fascinating excursion. Edinburgh is an hour or so's drive to the south.

THE GHOST is that of a Green Lady, who has spent years harassing occupants in one of the tower bedrooms.

She is one of the country's longest-known hotel ghosts, in that guests in the bedroom concerned started reporting disturbed nights back in Victorian times. The Green Lady did not appear to be malevolent, but she certainly started one or two staid Victorian visitors out of their nightcaps.

The hotel responded by turning the room into a staff bedroom. Undeterred, the Green Lady extended her territory to adjacent rooms – and sightings continued until quite recently. Then the hotel, tired of its uninvited guest, decided to have her exorcised and called in the local clergy. Bell, book and candle must have worked, because the Green Lady has not been seen since.

05 BALLYGALLY CASTLE Northern Ireland
Ballygally, Co. Antrim, Northern Ireland BT40 2QR
Telephone: 0574-83212
Fax: 0574-83681

> *Rooms:* include 4 double, 8 twin, 7 family
> *Location:* Quiet seaside   *Price Range:* ££
> *Restaurant:* à la carte ££; table d'hôte £
> *Facilities:* Historic building; tennis; fishing; gardens

Perched above the sea, amid lush green lawns, is the stone-built castle of Ballygally – now a country house hotel. The mellow castle buildings have the spires and turrets of a medieval French chateau – providing an overall effect known as Scottish Baronial.

The castle was built on the shores of Ballygally Bay by James Shaw in 1625, and its Scottish air is doubtless due to the Shaws' heritage – James was a descendant of Macduff, Thane of Fife, whose family was murdered by Macbeth in 834AD. The Shaws arrived in Antrim from Greenock in the early seventeenth century, and obtained land at Ballygally from the Earl of Antrim on very generous terms.

The result is today's historic and delightful Ballygally Castle Hotel. Despite its 5ft thick walls, slit windows and original carved stonework, the castle is a warm and welcoming building. The old and the new have been skilfully blended, and the original castle has been extended to include a former Georgian farmhouse and outbuildings, all of which now provide guest accommodation. Antique furniture from the eighteenth century decorates the lounge and lobby areas, and the hotel's pleasant restaurant has open views from its many windows. The menu is excellent, and has an international bias; but there is a strong emphasis on local ingredients and specialities, notably fresh fish.

The hotel's bar is an especially atmospheric corner: the dungeon where prisoners once languished has been converted into a low-ceilinged room with stone arches and oak beams, where guests can relax over a drink and the only 'racks' contain bottles of wine.

The hotel's 30 bedrooms, including the Antrim Suite with two bedrooms and lounge of its own, are pleasantly furnished in a modern style and have every comfort. But the beach-side hotel is in such a pleasant setting that guests may spend more time outdoors than in. For sportsmen, the hotel has its own trout stream, and there is good sea fishing nearby. Golf is available on several nearby courses.

Ballygally Castle is well situated as a touring base, handy for the ferry terminal at Larne, and within easy excursion distance of the beautiful Nine Glens of Antrim with their wooded walks, waterfalls and lovely scenery. Plenty of cottage crafts are still being carried on in the vicinity to tempt visitors into buying a unique local souvenir.

THE GHOST is in fact a trio of ghosts. Or perhaps even four. One visitor claims to have seen a whole group of them. On a bad night, Ballygally Castle can have more ghosts than guests! Chief ghost is probably Lady Shaw, a member of the original Scottish family who emigrated to Antrim in the early seventeenth century. She displeased her husband and he responded by locking her up and starving her. Eventually, Lady Shaw jumped to her death from a castle window, and it is she who is now thought to be responsible for the footsteps which are often heard crossing the dungeon which is now the hotel bar. Staff working late have often heard footsteps approaching the bar, turned to serve a prospective customer, and found no-one there. A night porter claims to have seen the ghost as well as hearing it.

But Ballygally's spirits aren't confined to the bar. Madame Nixon, an eighteenth-century worthy who gave her name to a local well and who – for reasons which are not clear – lived in the castle, still walks the corridors in a rustling silk dress. Occasionally she amuses herself by knocking on the bedroom doors.

If she knocks on the door of Room 1625 she could get a surprise, because – according to one American visitor – that has ghosts inside, too. A whole party of them. He banged on the door to complain about the noise coming from the room in the small hours, the door swung open, and he found himself confronted by a roomful of people in seventeenth-century costume. A fancy dress party? No, the management assured the American next morning; there were no groups staying in the hotel, and no-one staying in Room 1625 ....

In one of the castle's turret rooms, some guests have also reported odd experiences – like wardrobe doors opening and shutting of their own accord. One man who was reading a newspaper in bed accidentally dropped it on the floor. He leant over to pick it up, and found the pages being riffled by 'unseen hands'.

06 THE BEDFORD HOTEL West Country

1 Plymouth Road, Tavistock, nr Plymouth, Devon PL19 8BB
Telephone: 0822-613221
Fax: 0822-618034

> *Rooms:* include 13 double, 13 twin
> *Location:* Central   *Price Range:* ££
> *Restaurant:* The Woburn Restaurant (à la carte ££; table d'hôte £)
> *Facilities:* Business services

With its crenellated walls and arched entrance, the Bedford Hotel certainly lives up to its ancestry. It was built on the site of the tenth-century Tavistock Abbey, and rose from buildings demolished by the Duke of Bedford when he acquired the land after the Dissolution of the Monasteries in the sixteenth century. Of the original buildings, only a gateway can now be seen.

But the hotel, built in the eighteenth century, has its architectural compensations: the public rooms are in elegant Georgian style, with plasterwork ceilings and Gothic arches. The Bedford Bar has antique stained-glass windows shedding a warm glow over its cosy interior, and a range of light meals is available there at lunchtime. The Duke's Bar makes a peaceful venue for pre- or post-dinner drinks and the Woburn Restaurant, which overlooks

Tavistock Square and the lovely church, has a menu which is essentially English in flavour.

Each of the hotel's 30 bedrooms is decorated in a different style and colour scheme, to reflect that room's particular characteristics. Some have handsome drapes and matching quilted bedspreads; other feature antique furniture. But all have the modern amenities expected by today's visitors.

Tavistock is a pretty market town, with a commercial heritage that goes back more than six centuries. On the western fringes of Dartmoor, it makes an ideal base for touring the scenic National Park. Plymouth, with its naval heritage, is only 15 miles away, and Buckland Abbey – once a Cistercian monastery, later the home of the seafaring Grenville family, and bought by Sir Francis Drake in 1581 – is only a few minutes' drive away. Another monastery, Buckfast Abbey, a modern 'Gothic' building famous for the tonic wine still made by the monks, is also an interesting excursion.

THE GHOST is that of a young girl, and is seen walking through the Tower bedrooms, other bedrooms, the corridors – and even the restaurant.

Sightings are frequent, and when she appears in the Woburn Restaurant in front of a roomful of diners, it causes quite a stir. The girl's identity, however, remains a mystery.

But the Bedford Hotel is built on the remains of a tenth-century Benedictine Abbey, and local legend has it that the girl was the victim of a lecherous and villainous monk who promised to befriend her but then ravished her. Fearful of the consequences he then murdered the girl and disposed of her body – possibly in the vicinity of what is now the restaurant.

07 BEECHFIELD HOUSE   West Country

Beanacre, Melksham, Wiltshire SN12 7PU
Telephone: 0225-703700
Fax: 0225-790118

Rooms: 24 doubles/twins
Location: Rural   *Price Range:* £££
Restaurant: à la carte ££; table d'hôte £
Facilities: Tennis; croquet; heated outdoor pool; gardens.

This pale honey-coloured mansion, set in the midst of the Wiltshire countryside, was once the home of an affluent family of brewers. Built in 1878, Beechfield House keeps up the traditions of hospitality today, for it has become an intimate an luxurious country house hotel.

As you might expect, the Victorian space and comforts of the house have been very well converted to make Beechfield a delightful and restful place in which to stay. There is a variety of comfortable lounges, with views over the 8-acre gardens which provide much of the fruit, vegetables and herbs for the restaurant.

The dishes served in the restaurant are as elegant as the surroundings, and are delicious. The restaurant overlooks the fountain and walled garden, but on summer days there are barbecues around the hotel's swimming pool.

Roses ring the croquet lawn and tennis courts, and the lawns are shaded by magnificent old trees, including some mighty cedars.

The hotel's 24 bedrooms are named after the trees to be seen from their windows. Some are in the main house; others, like the four-poster-bedded Cedar Room, with its beamed ceiling, are in the former coach house. All the rooms are beautifully furnished with canopied beds and antiques, and the pretty chintzes tone with the room's individual colour schemes.

Beechfield House is in a quiet setting, but is convenient for the motorways. Bath, with its lovely architecture and Roman remains, not to mention its speciality shops, is a few minutes' drive away. There are many stately homes and historic places nearby like the picturesque National Trust village of Lacock, with its thirteenth-century abbey.

THE GHOST is that of an old woman, dressed in grey, identity unknown, who sits at the foot of a four-poster bed in one of the guest rooms in an annexe called the Old Coach House.

Trees press up against the windows of the room, the Magnolia Room, and give some odd light-and-shade effects in the daytime. The room itself has a high, open, beamed ceiling and is dominated by the ancient four-poster. Many guests have reported seeing the old lady either standing beside the bed or sitting at the foot of it – and there has been some speculation that she is attached to the bed rather than the room.

A regular visitor to Beechfield House, who had not heard these stories, returned to the hotel recently and was allocated the Magnolia Room. She immediately asked for her room to be changed, saying that this was the one room in the hotel where she could not sleep properly and was often disturbed. The manager confirms that guests have often said that the room has a 'creepy' feeling – and he agrees with this view.

Doors are often heard opening and closing in the main hotel building, even when no-one appears to be moving around, and the breakfast waitress had a very odd experience quite recently. Whilst changing for her shift, alone in the staff ladies' room at 6.30am, she heard a voice calling her by name. She responded, but discovered that no-one was there. The voice, she insisted, was that of an identifiable colleague – but it proved to be the colleague's day off.

Other members of the female staff have reported similar experiences – and always in the same place.

⃞08 THE BELL HOTEL   East Anglia

King Street, Thetford, Norfolk IP24 2AZ
Telephone: 0842-754455
Fax: 0842-755552

Rooms: include 15 double, 21 twin, 3 family rooms
Location: Central   *Price Range:* ££
Restaurant: à la carte £; table d'hôte £
    Chase Coffee Shop (light meals) £

Thetford is one of East Anglia's oldest market towns, complete with many timbered and flint buildings, and it has at its heart an old coaching inn, the Bell – its long, low, white facade laced with dark beams and looking very much as it must have done when it was built in the fifteenth century.

An imposing statue to one of the Thetford's most famous sons, Tom Paine, stands opposite the inn. He took up the cause of civil liberties in the eighteenth century, was involved in the American War of Independence, and wrote the highly controversial *Rights of Man*.

Tom Paine would still recognise many parts of the Bell Hotel: the Priory Bar, which retains its original walls, and the balcony, now walled in, which overlooks the coachyard. He might even recognise the low-ceilinged Chase Coffee Shop, which nowadays offers a range of grills and light meals throughout the day, besides having a special children's menu. The hotel's formal restaurant, decorated in elegant classical style, offers an international menu to match its up-market atmosphere.

Many of the hotel's 50 bedrooms are light and airy, with all conveniences, and there is a charming four-poster bedroom in one of the more historic parts of the building. Guests enjoy interesting views over the town and river.

Thetford is a pleasant town in which to stroll; the attractive streets contain the timbered Ancient House, the Tudor King's House, where King James I supposedly stayed, and the purpose-built gaol, a flint building erected in 1816.

But if the open spaces of the East Anglian countryside appeal, the Norfolk Broads are not far away, and Norwich, Bury St Edmunds with its Abbey, and Newmarket with its horse-racing, are within easy reach.

THE GHOST is that of Betty Radcliffe, who owned the inn in the eighteenth century. She died of a broken heart, and is often heard crying pitifully in one of the bedrooms.

Poor Betty was a comely wench, as the phraseology of the time had it. She ran a very successful inn, coping with the passengers from the 30 or 40 stage coaches a day as well as the locals who frequented the inn. And she ruled those who worked for her, in the kitchens, bars and stables, with a rod of iron.

But one day Betty took on a new ostler to help with the travellers' horses in the inn's vast stables. He was a handsome fellow and she fell in love with him. But the ostler could not see the merits of a match with the affluent and good-looking landlady, and rejected her. Betty became wild with grief and unrequited love.

Eventually, in 1750, in a fit of madness, she jumped to her death from the balcony of the inn, just outside the present Room 12.

Although the balcony has since been walled in, guests in Room 12, and in neighbouring rooms, have often reported heavy sighs and sobbing noises coming from an old wardrobe and carrying though the walls. Betty, it seems, cannot rest. She still anxiously paces the upper corridors of the hotel, where she has been seen as a shape with a bowed head and wringing its hands.

09 THE BERYSTEDE

Thames & Chilterns

Bagshot Road, Sunninghill, Ascot, Berkshire SL5 9JH
Telephone: 0344-23311
Fax: 0344-782301

Rooms: include 34 double, 33 twin
Location: Suburban but peaceful *Price Range:* £££££
Restaurant: à la carte £££; table d'hôte ££
Facilities: lift; gardens; swimming pool

A home of prestigious aspect and Gothic detail was what the Standish family had in mind when they built The Berystede in 1850. Set in the well-to-do 'merchant belt' of London's countryside, the house has cupolas and spires, turret rooms and mock-Tudor timbering, much of which was restored following a fire shortly after the house's completion.

King Edward VII, as Prince of Wales, was a frequent guest of the Standish family. But, despite their royal patronage, the family were not to enjoy their house for long: it passed from their hands in the early 1900s and has been a successful hotel ever since.

It is a warm, welcoming and elegant place. The sweeping oak staircase skirts the Oak Lounge and Library, which with their arches and pillars are both peaceful places to relax in. The balmy days of Queen Victoria's reign are also evident in the Hyperion Restaurant where, with a pianist playing during dinner, guests enjoy a very distinctive menu which has just the right touch of opulence. On Saturdays there is a real Palm Court feeling, as duettists play for dancing.

Most of the hotel's 91 bedrooms are modern, and are furnished to a very high international standard. But the rooms in the older part of the house, and especially those in the turrets, are more traditional, extremely elegant and furnished with antiques; some have four-poster beds. The curve of the turrets make for a delightful sitting area, with views over the nine acres of gardens and the surrounding countryside.

The Berystede has its own swimming pool, and the lawns and woodlands make for pleasant strolls. London is less than an hour away, and the attractive Berkshire countryside is all around. Windsor Castle and the River Thames are only a few minutes' drive away, and there is racing at Ascot, polo at Smith's Lawn and golf on the top-class course at Wentworth.

THE GHOST is that of Eliza, a lady's maid who died in a devastating fire in the late nineteenth century. She is often seen in the corridors outside the bedrooms in the older part of the hotel, apparently searching for something.

Eliza was the servant of one of the distinguished house-guests who went to stay with the Standish family at their new home, now The Berystede Hotel. It was she who discovered the fire, and, after alerting her mistress and the other guests, she left the building for the safety of the gardens.

But, as flames roared through the lovely wood-panelled rooms, Eliza suddenly remembered her jewellery, treasured possessions given to her by a previous employer in gratitude for good service. Ignoring all calls for her to be sensible and stay outside, Eliza rushed back to the bedroom she had occupied beside that of her mistress, grabbed her jewel-box, and ran for the stairs.

But she was too late; fire had engulfed the exits and Eliza was trapped. She died in the flames, and her body was later discovered surrounded by the charred and melted bracelets and neck-chains, brooches and rings which she valued more than life itself.

She values them still. For Eliza has often been seen by staff and guests, wearing a long white nightgown and searching the corridor floor for her jewellery.

⑩ THE BLACK SWAN HOTEL

Yorkshire & Humberside

Market Place, Helmsley, Yorkshire YO6 5BJ
Telephone: 0439-70466
Fax: 0439-70174

Rooms: include 23 double, 18 twin
Location: Central   *Price Range:* ££££
Restaurant: à la carte ££; table d'hôte £
Facilities: Historic building; gardens

Looking like the country inn it has been for most of its life, the Black Swan at Helmsley is now a luxurious hotel with a delightful mixture of buildings in varying architectural styles. Its simplicity and rural charm are emphasised by the masses of climbing roses that wreath the doors and windows of the honey-coloured stone frontage.

The main part of the hotel is Elizabethan, restyled in Georgian times: but its roots go back even farther. The Tudor House annexe to the hotel, separating it from the church, was once a priory and later the rectory: it is a chocolate-box black and white timbered building under a warm red-tiled roof.

Inside, the hotel is far removed from a country pub as far as elegance and comfort are concerned. The lovely beams and woodwork of yesteryear have been preserved; the huge fireplaces, one with vast copper hood and brick niches; the china and knick-knacks everywhere; and the prints and pretty chintzes, all give a remarkably cosy ambience, with a feeling of being wrapped around England's history.

That atmosphere is heightened by the caring staff, and the general excellence of the service: a quietly efficient and friendly team run the hotel, and nothing is too much trouble.

The restaurant has an excellent reputation: the food is that individual blend of English best and international haute cuisine that is gaining fame, and the Black Swan's gourmet meals are very tempting. Meals are served in the elegant Georgian-style dining-room with its carved fireplace, and drinks are served in the Garden Lounge, overlooking the hotel's colourful walled garden.

The 44 bedrooms include spacious suits, but all the rooms are furnished to a very high standard of comfort, with luxurious touches in the furnishings. They have all the expected modern amenities, and feature period furniture among the antiques and pretty drapes.

Helmsley is a pretty market town on the edge of the moors, and has a number of interesting places to visit nearby: Rievaulx Abbey for example, and the magnificent stately home of Castle Howard. York is only a short drive away, and there is horse-racing at Beverley.

THE GHOST is that of a wayward child, who is heard – but sometimes just sensed – in two of the bedrooms in the Tudor House part of the hotel.

The spirit is thought to be that of a very young child, whose remains were found concealed in the chimney breast between Rooms 15 and 16, in a part of the hotel which has in its time been both a priory and a rectory. Who the child was, and how it came to be in the chimney, is a mystery. One theory is that it crawled up in play and suffocated.

Strange noises have always been reported in this part of the building, both before and after the discovery of the body many years ago. But just lately the spirit has become unusually active – with guests in those two rooms reporting disturbed nights as frequently as once a fortnight. In April 1991 there were three separate occurrences. The last of these resulted in a regular guest, a school teacher named Miss Sims, who had heard of the spirit's activities, blessing the rooms.

'Disruptive' is how visitors have reported the spirit. They have awakened to hear a variety of crying, laughing or screaming noises – and sometimes all three – coming from various parts of the two rooms. 'Just as if the child were having a tantrum and rampaging about', said hotel housekeeper Annie Collier, who had to relocate one couple after a noisy night in Room 16. 'But it's definitely not frightening.'

Other guests have reported feeling that someone was watching them at night, as they were asleep, or sitting in the lounge area of their room. One young wife awoke to find her husband apparently fighting something unseen that was pinning him to the bed. He was not asleep or dreaming, but could not say afterwards what had been affecting him. Sadly, the ghost remains completely quiet when guests book into Room 16 in the specific hope of experiencing something supernatural.

Annie Collier has slept in both rooms on many occasions in her twelve years with the hotel, and she too has experienced nothing.

11 BORINGDON HALL — West Country

Colebrook, Plympton, Plymouth, Devon PL7 4DP
Telephone: 0752-344455
Fax: 0752-346578

Rooms: 10 double, 40 double/twin
Location: Rural   *Price Range:* ££££
Restaurant: Gallery (international, à la carte ££; table d'hôte £);
    Admiral's Carvery £
Facilities: Historic building; lift; tennis; pitch-and-putt; gardens

If a building has been, in turn, monastery and manor house then it is used to entertaining guests. Boringdon Hall, now a country house hotel, has moved with the times – but still maintains its traditions of hospitality.

Boringdon Hall

The medieval monastery, close to Plymouth itself, and founded about 1,000 years ago, was eventually presented to the Earl of Southampton by King Henry VIII. The house was remodelled into the height of Elizabethan fashion and comfort by John Parker, who entertained both his friend Sir Francis Drake, and Queen Elizabeth I, there. The Parker family, loyal to the Crown, briefly lost Boringdon Hall to Cromwell during the Civil Wars, but their loyalty was rewarded with lands and wealth at the restoration of King Charles II. The Parkers celebrated by moving to a larger and more up-to-date house and the Hall went into a decline. But now it has been rescued and lovingly restored by the Maund family, who have made it into an attractive as well as an historic place at which to stay.

The Hall has as its heart the original timbered Great Hall, now the lounge. This room features a vast fireplace and marble overmantel, a minstrels' gallery and arched doorways leading to some of the many sitting-out places furnished with antiques. On a balcony, overlooking the hall, is the Gallery restaurant, a romantic place to dine with a menu featuring English cuisine. For a less formal meal there is the Admiral's Carvery.

Boringdon Hall's original bedrooms – ten stone chambers in the old house – are furnished with Elizabethan four-poster beds and antique furniture. But they do not lack for mod cons either – and the twentieth century is present in the shape of satellite TV. The new wing has 40 spacious rooms with a blend of modern and period furnishings.

The gardens and grounds are lovely throughout the year and have a pitch-and-putt course and tennis courts for guests. Dartmoor and the Devon coast are within easy reach, with the sailing centre of the South Hams a magnet for enthusiasts. Plymouth and Dartmouth are both worth a visit.

THE GHOST is that of a serving maid, wearing Tudor dress, who is often seen wandering distraught in the upper corridors of the old house.

In the fifteenth century, Boringdon Hall was the home of Lady Jane Grey's family, through her connection with the Earl of Southampton. Lady Jane Grey stayed at the Hall at times during her short life: she died on the block at the Tower of London in 1554, beheaded for her part in a struggle for the throne. Rebels led by the Earl of Southampton had proclaimed her Queen; but her reign lasted only nine days.

It is thought that the serving maid who still walks the staircase and corridors of Boringdon Hall had the job of waiting on Lady Jane during her visits and grew very fond of her. But she foresaw her mistress's fate, and the spectral maid is always weeping, covering her face with her hands. Her appearances, always preceded by a sharp drop in temperature, are thought to herald some disaster for the Hall or its owners.

Most recently, she was seen by the last owner – and her appearance was followed by a costly fire at the Hall. Feeling that she had been warning him, and that he had disregarded the warning, he sold the Hall some twelve years ago.

She has not been reported since, and present owners Robert and Maureen Maund are glad not to have made her acquaintance. Whether or not they would pay heed to her warning is something they keep to themselves.

12 BOSWORTH HALL   East Midlands

The Park, Market Bosworth, near Nuneaton,
Leicestershire CV13 0LP
Telephone: 0455-291919
Fax: 0455-292442

> *Rooms:* include 28 double, 44 twin, 2 family rooms
> *Location:* Rural   *Price Range:* £££££
> *Restaurant:* à la carte ££; table d'hôte £
> *Facilities:* Historic building; lift; extensive grounds

King Richard III lost his crown on the edge of this hotel's gardens. A clump of elms marks the spot where the king raised his standard before the fateful battle of Bosworth Field in 1485. In the aftermath of the battle, and under the victorious Tudors, the half-timbered Bosworth Hall became the home of the Dixie family, and it was they who built the imposing hall in the 1680s.

Bosworth Hall

Over the centuries, the house has seen many comings and goings through its filigree iron gates and across the bridge over the moat. Some visitors, surely, hastened their departure at the sight of the eccentric nineteenth-century traveller Lady Florence Dixie exercising her pet jaguar, 'Affums', in the gardens. In the 1880s another owner, Charles Tollemache Scott, installed iron gates from Newgate Prison in the wine cellars: perhaps he feared the butler's light fingers.

These gates, and many more architectural delights, await guests at Bosworth Hall today. A newly extended and impressive 185-bedroomed country house hotel, the Hall has a wonderful elaborately-carved staircase, its baskets of fruit and flowers echoed in the panelling of the state rooms. Beamed and carved ceilings give a regal air to the entrance hall, with its massive stone fireplace, and the elegant drawing-room. There are many murals depicting classical scenes, and looking as fresh today as when they were painted.

The Victorian-style Dining Room, its wide windows opening on to the terrace and gardens, offers a wide-ranging menu of English and French dishes. And the wine list has some special treats, perhaps protected by those prison gates.

The six bedrooms in the original house reflect Victorian opulence: their historic carved beds include some impressive four-poster beds, and the drapes have a distinctive nineteenth-century richness. The bathrooms rejoice in cast-iron claw-footed baths and antique-style washstands with gleaming brass fitments. The rooms in the new wings are in keeping, with many period touches, and are equipped to a luxurious standard.

Bosworth Hall's park is a lovely place to stroll in. But if visitors feel they must escape to the outside world, then the up-to-date motor sport centres of Donington Park and Mallory Park are nearby, as is the grand theme park at Alton Towers. Market Bosworth itself is of interest because it is almost the geographic centre of England.

THE GHOST is that of Anna Dixie, a young lady who died a terrible death in the ground of Bosworth Hall. She still roams the house and gardens on her way to the lovers' tryst that cost her her life.

Anna was the daughter of the original owner, Sir Wolstan Dixie, who was Lord Mayor of London in 1585. She fell in love with a local yeoman farmer, but her father felt that the farmer was 'beneath' her and forbade the lovers to meet. The couple defied his orders, and continued to meet secretly in the depths of the park.

But the girl's maid spied on them, and told Anna's father what was going on. Determined to have his own way, Sir Wolstan responded by having a number of man-traps placed about the park, in the path of the young man.

But his plan misfired. It was not the yeoman farmer who fell foul of a man-trap one dark night but Anna herself. She was severely wounded by the trap's iron teeth, developed gangrene, and died in agony several days later.

Full of remorse, her father gave her a lavish burial. But poor Anna cannot rest and is often seen as a grey shape roaming the entrance hall, pausing by the main doors, then passing though them even when they are closed and locked for the night. She then drifts across the moat and into the park – endlessly repeating her last dreadful walk.

13 BRADFORD OLD WINDMILL

West Country

Masons Lane, Bradford-on-Avon, Wiltshire BA15 1QN
Telephone: 02216-6842

Rooms: 4 double
Location: Suburban but peaceful *Price Range:* £
Restaurant: vegetarian table d'hote by arrangement only: £
Facilities: Unusual building; gardens

It is rather appropriate for an old windmill, which now offers exceptionally comfortable bed-and-breakfast accommodation, to be a vegetarian house. Bradford Old Windmill, which has been very imaginatively converted to offer guest accommodation, offers its visitors delicious evening meals by arrangement – always following vegetarian principles.

Peter and Priscilla Roberts have carefully extended and converted the old windmill, retaining its ancient character. Windows are arched and rather Gothic, the homely lounge is circular, and the rather pretty furnishings have all been imaginatively designed to fit the awkward angles of such an atmospheric building. Natural fabrics and wood predominate, blending with the old stone walls to make a home of great charm and comfort.

The mill's four guest bedrooms are warm and cosy and one, like the lounge, is completely circular. All have en suite facilities – no mean achievement in such a unique building. Two are large enough to be used as family rooms, and all enjoy spectacular views over the picturesque town of Bradford-on-Avon.

Bradford-on-Avon has one of the best Saxon churches in the country among its pretty streets, and the bridge chapel is one of the very few in England. The Georgian city of Bath – where Roman remains and luxury shops exist side by side – is only a short drive away, and the lovely Cotswold villages are nearby. There is an American Museum at Claverton, just 12 miles away, housing a collection of American art and early furniture. Also worth a visit: the National Trust House of Dyrham Park.

THE GHOST is that of a dog which was abandoned by a bankrupt miller and left chained to a tree. It is often heard whining and rattling its chain at night, in the gardens of the Old Windmill.

Thomas Smart, a local baker, bought the mill in the early nineteenth century to grind his own flour. The enterprise failed, and the mill was abandoned. But in quitting his ill-fated enterprise, the not-so-smart Mr Smart left his faithful dog chained to an apple tree in the yard. It died of starvation.

You don't believe such stories? Well, when the present owners, Peter and Priscilla Chapman, were excavating to build new rooms at the mill, the builder's' machinery unearthed the stump of an old tree in the grounds. Attached to it was a length of rusty chain. And at the end of the chain, its neck through the loop, was the skeleton of a dog.

The dog is heard on dark and windy nights, rattling its chain –

despite the fact that there are no metal objects nearby to account for the noise. Animal lovers among the guests have found it very distressing, and the Chapmans' cat shares their feelings: it will not go near the site of the old apple tree.

The Chapmans have tried laying the ghost. They have brought the bones indoors, and kept them safe – and have even given the dog a name: 'Ben'. But Ben's chain still rattles outside the windmill as he tries in vain to free himself.

14 BRANDSHATCH PLACE S E England

Fawkham, Kent DA3 8NQ
Telephone: 0474-872239
Fax: 0474-879652

> *Rooms:* include 18 double, 9 twin
> *Location:* Rural but convenient   *Price Range:* £££
> *Restaurant:* in main hotel: à la carte ££; table d'hôte £
>   Fredericks (coffee shop and pub style): £
> *Facilities:* Lift; sports and leisure centre; gardens

In 1806, the then Duke of Norfolk fancied building himself a country cottage, and the red-brick Georgian house at Brandshatch Place was the result. But it's a cottage of ducal proportions, with 29 bedrooms and set in 12 acres of grounds at the end of a long wooded drive.

Recently the 'cottage' has been extended and refurbished to make it one of the most delightful country club-style hotels in Britain. The lounges and bar are furnished in period style, in tones which the Duke would have admired: the bar, for instance, is in a soft Georgian green. And there is a spacious, peaceful feeling throughout; a feeling to which the unobtrusive staff contribute by their calm efficiency.

The restaurant, overlooking the lovely gardens, prides itself on its menu of English dishes, created with a special light touch which adds opulence without any trace of Regency over-indulgence.

The bedrooms are beautiful, their pale tones adding to the

feeling of peace and space. Some rooms have four-poster beds, and one has a magnificent brass canopy bed. All have every modern amenity.

The country club, 'Fredericks', has something for visitors of any age – from squash, badminton, tennis and a gym to a playroom with playbricks and a creche. There are plenty of health and beauty treatments there too, including an indoor swimming pool and whirlpool spa bath. If all that exercise has made you peckish, there's no need to go back to the main hotel for refreshments: Fredericks has a conservatory-style lounge serving light refreshments and a traditional English pub-style bar with its own menu.

The delightful Kent countryside is all around, and the pretty town of Sevenoaks is only a short drive away. The motor-racing circuit at Brands Hatch is on the doorstep; by contrast the historic Hever Castle and the lovely Leeds Castle make interesting excursions.

THE GHOST is that of Mollie, a young housekeeper at Brandshatch Place in Edwardian times, who suddenly disappeared without trace. She is frequently seen walking though the doors from the kitchen to the garden.

Mollie was young and pretty, and worked at Brandshatch Place in its heyday as a private house. Her employer was a bachelor, and it is thought that the lively Mollie caught his eye. But when his clandestine attachment to his below-stairs lady-love became known to others, he is supposed to have removed her from the house – permanently. How he disposed of her, and whether he murdered her or paid her to disappear, is not known. Mollie was simply never seen again.

But, in the years following her disappearance, other servants at Brandshatch Place reported sighting her in her old domain – the housekeeper's room in what is now the hotel's reception area. Recently hotel managers and staff have met her as they go about their work.

In 1990, she was seen twice by staff, passing through the reception hall and then in the kitchen on her way to the garden. She is always nearly dressed in a long, straight-skirted gown with an apron, and carrying a basket of flowers.

Her preoccupation with the garden is puzzling. Was it a favourite place in her lifetime? Or is there a more sinister reason connected with the real Mollie's last resting-place?

15 BROWNSOVER HALL — Heart of England

Brownsover Lane, Old Brownsover, Rugby,
Warwickshire CV21 1HU
Telephone: 0788-546100
Fax: 0788-579241

Rooms: include 15 double, 5 twin, 2 family rooms
Location: Rural   *Price Range:* ££££
Restaurant: à la carte ££; table d'hôte £
Facilities: Extensive grounds

Near Rugby stands the awesome Brownsover Hall. Built in Gothic style by Gilbert Scott in the late eighteenth century, and looking rather like some of the nation's grander railway stations, the Hall comes complete with a tower, a spire, and arched windows with stone tracery. It is an imposing building of patterned red brick, and is set in seven acres of lovely grounds.

The original hall was constructed in the 1450s, and has spent most of its time in the hands of the Broughton-Leigh family. Today, their Gothic pile is the handsome and stylish Brownsover Hall hotel.

The reception area is also a comfortable sitting room, with well-upholstered day beds and easy chairs. Above the massive stone fireplace is an even more massive set of antlers, a trophy of some male Broughton's hunting expeditions. There are antiques and objets d'art everywhere, adding to the nineteenth-century baronial atmosphere.

The Scott restaurant overlooks the three-acre formal garden and offers an extensive menu. It is furnished in period style. The lovely bay windows make delightful alcoves in which to enjoy the international-style cuisine. The original Library and Drawing Room, which retain their magnificence and atmospheric decor, are used for private functions.

There are 31 bedrooms, all with luxurious fabrics and period furniture. They are very spacious and have individual colour schemes as well as every modern amenity. Many enjoy lovely views.

The estate has much unspoilt woodland, and there are riverside walks to tempt guests out for a stroll. Rugby itself, only a few miles away, is where the game of rugby football originated in the 1820s. Stratford-upon-Avon, with its Shakespearean connections, is only a short drive away.

THE GHOST is that of 'One-Handed Broughton' – a larger-than-life member of the family which owned the Hall in the nineteenth century.

Nobody seems too sure of his real name, but One-Handed Broughton was, as his melodramatic nickname suggests, a drinker and brawler who lost his hand in a fight. Undeterred by his handicap, he continued his ebullient lifestyle – but also became an overbearing and unpopular proprietor of the estate in his turn.

It is probable that few mourned his passing. But, if you believe the local stories, he hasn't gone! They say that he still careers about the grounds in a phantom coach pulled by six horses, apparently indulging in a drunken race with unseen friends.

The Bull Hotel, Peterborough

16 THE BULL HOTEL East Anglia

Westgate, Peterborough, Cambridgeshire PE1 1RB
Telephone: 0733-61364
Telex: 987176

Rooms: include 25 double, 19 twin, 3 family
Location: Central   *Price Range:* ££
Restaurant: The Knights Room (à la carte ££; table d'hôte £)
   Coffee Shop (light meals) £
Facilities: Lift

What do the Queen Mother, the Emperor of Japan, and film star Lee Marvin have in common? The answer is that they have all stayed in the Wakeford Suite of the Bull Hotel, just a stone's throw from Peterborough Cathedral.

The hotel, one of the nicest things in this booming city, is an old coaching inn dating back in part to the fourteenth century. Now it has been extended and beautifully modernised to provide 112 bedrooms and extensive public rooms – the latter all furnished with original oil paintings and antiques.

The oldest part of the hotel, fronting the Westgate, houses a bar with deep vaulted alcoves and a coffee-shop lounge which has a beautiful Georgian plasterwork ceiling – just one of several such ceilings in the hotel. Perhaps the most impressive of these ceilings is the dark, carved and gilded one in the reception room known as the Cardinal Suite.

The Knights Room restaurant lies in the centre of the hotel, and comes as quite a contrast to the tapestries and old oak elsewhere: it is light with cane furniture, palms and ceiling fans, and has been modelled on the famous Raffles Hotel in Singapore. Its menu is extensive, and the table d'hote dinner is excellent value. And there's usually an authentic Italian dish or two.

The hotel's two guest suites – the first floor Wakeford Suite and its twin immediately above it – are modern but impressively furnished. Generally speaking, bedrooms in the older part of the hotel are more spacious, but all are pleasantly furnished in individual colour schemes, and have many nice period touches – not to mention the antiques scattered everywhere. There are family rooms, too. And the hotel has plans for a swimming pool and leisure centre in the near future.

The Bull is a very busy hotel, but it is very well run and the staff are friendly and helpful.

A series of secret passages is said to run across the street to Peterborough Cathedral, but these are not open to the public. Nevertheless the Cathedral, the oldest Norman cathedral in Britain, should not be missed on any visit to the city. Peterborough also has superb shopping, and the under-cover Queensgate Centre is right opposite the hotel. Touring possibilities include market towns of East Anglia, the fenland wildlife in reserves like the gardens at Peakirk, and the Nene Valley Steam Railway.

THE GHOST is of an old lady dressed in white – identity unknown – who has been seen by both staff and guests and who, extraordinarily, is always accompanied by an equally ghostly small white dog.

Most sightings have been in what is now the hotel's coffee shop, to the right of the entrance hall. This used to be the public bar, and is the oldest part of the building – perhaps dating back to the fourteenth century and certainly the fifteenth century.

But the old lady has also been spotted in the bedroom right

above the coffee shop: the Wakeford Suite. The suite is the best room in the house and has a comfortable and welcoming atmosphere, and none of the Bull's famous overnight guests has ever reported anything out of the ordinary. But some guests say they have seen an old lady and her dog disappearing through the bedroom wall and into the next room, and one visitor refused to sleep in the suite.

The old lady seems to be shy: business guests have often staged all-night vigils in the coffee shop in an attempt to spot her, but no such ghost hunt has ever succeeded. Manager Ashor Osib, who has worked at The Bull for 16 years, has never seen her either. But before the public bar was turned into a coffee shop, the barmaid saw her twice.

The most dramatic sighting, however, was fairly recently when the then night porter, David Cherry, spotted an old lady with long hair and a long white dress standing at the top of the steps which lead from the hotel's reception area into the hotel bar and coffee shop. She had a small white dog with her, and seemed quite tangible.

Because it was 3am, the night porter thought she must be a trespasser who had wandered in from the street, and he approached her and asked if there was anything he could do. She smiled at him, then turned and walked down the steps. David Cherry followed – and was amazed to see the old lady and her dog disappear through the old, and very solid, wall.

Most such sightings in the small hours are easily dismissed by sceptics. But on this occasion the night porter had a colleague with him, and the pair had no hesitation in calling the police. The police searched the hotel, with dogs, for the mysterious 'intruder' but found not a sniff of her!

⑰ THE BULL HOTEL

East Anglia

Hall Street, Long Melford, Sudbury, Suffolk CO10 9JG
Telephone: 0787-378494
Fax: 0787-880307

Rooms: include 15 double, 7 twin
Location: Central but peaceful   *Price Range:* £££
Restaurant: à la carte ££; table d'hôte £
Facilities: Historic building

East Anglia was once the most densely populated part of Britain – and possibly the wealthiest. The timber-framed Bull Hotel, in the Suffolk village of Long Melford, is proof of that wealth, for this spacious and beautiful building, erected in 1450, was originally the home of a prosperous wool merchant.

Just over 100 years later, the house became the Bull Inn, and was busy with the passenger coaches that plied between London and

Norwich. Now, much in this lovely house is still as it was then – the rooms have open beams, some with carved mouldings, others bleached pale by time or darkened by smoke, and the studwork walls have been opened to make a number of delightful sitting places.

The Drawing Room and Bar have vast Elizabethan fireplaces, and the Cordell Room restaurant, with its broad-linteled fireplace with copper hood and oak settles, serves a menu that is intended to give local specialities an international flavour.

The hotel's 25 bedrooms are beautifully furnished, as are the downstairs rooms, with a blend of period furniture and pretty modern fabrics. Some of the rooms in the newer parts of the building have little sitting areas in arched alcoves, while in one memorable room there is a timbered room-within-a-room sheltering the bed behind rich drapes. All the bedrooms are very comfortable and have all mod. cons.

The hotel's courtyard makes a cool and pleasant place to sit on a summer's evening; it is overlooked by the old weavers' gallery that runs along at first-floor level.

The village of Long Melford has a long main street – hence its name – bordered by thatched cottages and many more timbered buildings. Melford Hall, a National Trust house, is only a short walk away, and has an excellent collection of paintings and furniture. The other Suffolk 'wool towns' – Lavenham with its medieval Guildhall, Clare and Cavendish with their vineyards, and Kersey with its watersplash – are an easy drive away, so the Bull makes a fine base for a fascinating tour into the 'real' England. What is more, the lovely countryside around Dedham and Flatford immortalised by painter John Constable is within an hour's drive.

THE GHOST is that of Richard Evered, who was stabbed to death in the hallway of the Bull in July 1648. He is thought to be responsible for moving furniture around and slamming doors in an unused bedroom of the hotel which is kept locked and empty.

Richard was a yeoman farmer, who used to frequent the Bull Inn, as it was then, for business as well as pleasure. One summer's evening he called in for a tankard or two of the Bull's excellent ale.

Whether Richard or his drinking partner, Roger Green, had a tankard too many that night is not known. But the two men's discussions became increasingly acrimonious, and Roger Green finally lost his temper and drew a knife. Plunging it into Richard Evered's chest, he fled – leaving his supposed friend for dead on the hall floor.

The body was laid out in what is now the hotel lounge. But come the dawn, there was no corpse to be found. A local legend says that Green sneaked back and disposed of the evidence against him by getting rid of the body. Certainly the corpse was never recovered.

Shortly afterwards, guests in a room above the hall began complaining of furniture being mysteriously moved, and doors slamming of their own accord. Eventually, no-one would sleep in the room and it was sealed.

It remains sealed and empty to this day. Visitors to the inn still hear the sound of doors slamming. And no-one has yet volunteered to sleep in the sealed room.

18 BURGH ISLAND   West Country

Bigbury-on-Sea, South Devon TQ7 4AU
Telephone: 0548-810514

Rooms: 9 double, 4 twin
Location: Offshore, rural   *Price Range:* ££££ *(includes dinner)*
Restaurant: extensive table d'hôte
Facilities: Tennis; snooker; table tennis; extensive grounds

'Getting away from it all' takes on a new meaning at Burgh Island. Is it an hotel? Is it a resort? Is it a step back in time? Whatever you may call it, this lovely island off the coast of Devon is cut off from the outside world by the tide twice a day.

Once a monastic community, then a sparsely settled fishing community, and finally a mecca of the jazz and swing eras of the 1920s and 1930s, the island and its Art Deco hotel fell into disrepair after the Second World War. But the hotel was rescued, and lovingly restored to its original glamorous state, by enthusiasts

Tony and Bea Porter.

Today the island experience, which inspired the scenes in many an Agatha Christie thriller, is open to guests and offers a unique 'time capsule' stay in its 13 suites. The Burgh Island Hotel has been described as a 'Temple to Art Deco'. The foyer gleams with black glass and pink mirrors; the Palm Court, with its glass Peacock Dome, is a stunningly elegant cocktail lounge; and the Ballroom, with its own orchestra, is now the dining room. Here the varied menus include fish caught by the hotel's own fisherman – including crab, pilchards and lobster – and of course Devon clotted cream.

Breakfast is served in the curious setting of the old Captain's Cabin of *HMS Ganges* built in 1820 and saved from the breaker's yard by the hotel's owner in the 1930s. It was eventually attached rather haphazardly to the front of the building. On a moonlit night, it can look rather eerie!

Wherever you look, Tony and Bea Porter have striven to recreate the authentic feeling of the Roaring Twenties. They have replaced the original furniture – destroyed in a mad beach bonfire by a former owner – with genuine period pieces. The bedrooms are all vast, have their own sitting rooms, contain wonderful period furnishings, and are blessed with wide windows – some with balconies or terraces – from which to enjoy the views.

There is no need to leave the island for recreation: there are walks, wildlife preserves, beaches, and a natural rock swimming pool at Mermaid Cove. Tennis courts, snooker and table tennis are provided by the hotel. The island itself covers 26 acres, and even has its own pub, the Pilchard Inn, dating from the fourteenth century and now serving bistro meals.

Access to the island is by a massive sea-tractor, riding high above the incoming tides. Guests must leave their cars on the mainland and time their arrival for low tide, for the tractor can make the crossing only then. Leaving the island to sample the delights of mainland Devon needs equally careful planning – so it is probably just as well that Burgh Island is so self-contained.

THE GHOST of Burgh Island is, fittingly, a fisherman and smuggler, Tom Crocker. He walks the island, near the Pilchard Inn which was his headquarters, and on misty nights there are said to be strange happenings near the inn.

Tom seems to date back to the sixteenth century, and led the customs officers a merry dance. The island, which he used as his base, has his lair in a cliff-bound cave, a secret passage down to the sea, a secret hoard to treasure, and tells tales of his death at the hands of one of the Crown excise men determined to end Tom's smuggling activities.

If you spot his hazy figure creeping along a cliff path, you'll be sure to recognise him, for his effigy is to be seen beside the fireplace in the Pilchard Inn where he planned his escapades over a tankard of ale.

But the island has other mysterious inhabitants. There is evidence of a religious past in the ruined chapel which tops the highest point of the island, and a monastery once occupied the site of the present hotel. One of the monks obviously did not want to tear himself away from this lovely spot, for his ghost has been reported near the chapel and the old 'huer's hut' on the hill where the fishermen kept watch for shoals.

19 THE CASTLE HOTEL   Wales

High Street, Conwy, Gwynedd LL32 8DB, Wales
Telephone: 0492-592324
Fax: 0492-583351

Rooms: include 11 double, 11 twin, 2 family rooms
Location: Central   *Price Range:* £££
Restaurant: à la carte £; table d'hôte £

Right in the heart of Conwy, lying at the foot of the medieval castle from which it takes its name, the Castle Hotel has a tradition dating back – like its building – to the fifteenth century.

Its Jacobean-style facade hides some remains of that older building as well as a wealth of Georgian rooms where guests have been entertained in the comfort through the decades. One guest, a penniless painter called John Dawson-Watson, enjoyed his stay so much that when he ran out of funds he offered to paint pictures for

The Castle Hotel, Conwy

the hotel in lieu of his bill. Surprisingly, the then-proprietors agreed – and the result is a series of handsome paintings dating from the 1890s which hang on the hotel's walls. One, a hunting scene, is unfinished: the artist came into an inheritance and left in a hurry.

The lounge and restaurant, named after Shakespeare, are full of curios and antiques, and the bar is a popular spot with visitors and local people alike. The Shakespeare Restaurant specialises in seafood, with locally-caught fish, especially mussels and salmon, as principal ingredients.

The hotel's 29 bedrooms, all with modern comforts, are very pleasantly decorated but the star of them all has a vast, massively-carved oak four-poster bed which bears the ominous legend: 'God help me through the night'.

Overlooking the Menai Straits and the island of Anglesey, Conwy Castle is a splendid viewpoint over the Vale of Conwy and the three bridges spanning the river and estuary full of fishing boats. The town also boasts that it has the 'smallest house in Britain', plus a seventeenth-century watermill in working order. The climate is said to be unusually mild.

Snowdonia – with its mountains, wildlife and industrial heritage – is on the doorstep. The city of Chester, with its medieval walls and 'Rows' of galleried shops, is nearby, as are the seaside resorts of Llandudno and Colwyn Bay.

THE GHOST is that of a chambermaid at the hotel, who more than 100 years ago sickened and died of a broken heart. Or perhaps the occurrences attributed to the girl should be more correctly ascribed to 'George' – for the things that happen in the hotel, all without any apparent human agency or other natural explanation, are rather more masculine in nature.

Ever since the death of the poor chambermaid, for the love of a local fisher lad, during the nineteenth century, there have been mysterious and sometimes irritating goings-on in various parts of the hotel: guests' possessions being moved around, lights going on and off, and things being 'lost' then reappearing in places where they could not have been overlooked.

It seems that the chambermaid, almost willing herself into her grave, repeatedly told other staff that she wanted to be buried in the churchyard near her home on the island of Anglesey. But the owner of the Castle at that time was unsympathetic, and did not want either the expense or the trouble of a long-distance funeral. So, when the maid died, he had her body laid to rest in the nearest churchyard.

But, apparently she did not rest – and poltergeist activity kept up until she was returned to Anglesey, as she had requested, some years later.

However, the odd happenings at the hotel did not altogether cease. If anything, they took a turn for the worse. Now a mischievous spirit, known familiarly as 'George', loves to fill ashtrays with water and turn off the gas supply to the beer barrels in the cellar.

It's a source of great amusement to the guests. The staff, who have to clear up after 'George', do not always find it so funny.

20 THE CASTLE HOTEL — West Country

Castle Green, Taunton, Somerset TA1 1NF
Telephone: 0823-272671
Fax: 0823-336066

Rooms: include 11 double, 11 twin
Location: Central   *Price Range:* ££££
Restaurant: à la carte ££; table d'hôte ££
Facilities: Historic building

The guest list of the Castle Hotel, which dates back to Norman times, reads like a *Who's Who* of history: 'big name' guests at this beautiful hotel over the centuries have included King John, medieval rebel leader Perkin Warbeck, the 'Bloody Assizes' Judge Jeffreys, the Duke of Wellington, poet Samuel Taylor Coleridge and Victorian politician and author Benjamin Disraeli. Any number of other royal and VIP guests have enjoyed the Castle's hospitality in more recent times.

The wisteria-clad seventeenth-century facade, with its Gothic-style gatehouse and portcullis, hides many beautiful rooms. The elegant restaurant, in Georgian style, is softly lit by brass

The Castle Hotel, Taunton

candelabra and serves the very special dishes that have won the hotel much acclaim in food circles: the best of local ingredients with a nouvelle cuisine touch. The lounge and bar are extremely comfortable and full of antique detail, and are very pleasant places in which to sit and relax. But it is the staff and their caring attitude which set the seal on the overall excellence of the Castle Hotel and ensure its well-deserved reputation.

The 35 bedrooms are all lavishly furnished in a timeless and gracious English style, with wide beds, deep armchairs, period furniture and pictures, and pretty chintz fabrics. Four of the rooms are known as garden suites, and enjoy lovely views over the hotel's unique Norman Garden in which ancient stone walls provide a mellow backdrop for cottage-garden flowers.

The Chapman family, who have owned and run the Castle Hotel for two generations, have an immense pride in this lovely and very special hotel.

If guests do manage to tear themselves away, there is much to see and do in the area, for – although it is in the town centre – the Castle is set amid lovely countryside close to the rolling Exmoor landscape that inspired R.D. Blackmore to write *Lorna Doone*. For devotees of Thomas Hardy, 'his' country is only a short drive away too; as are the lovely villages and coast of Devon.

THE GHOST is a very romantic one. And it is never seen, only heard. From somewhere in the depths of the building, only occasionally and only when few people are around to hear, there comes the sad sound of violins.

No tangible cause for the music has ever been found, nor is there any legend connected with the hotel which would explain the violins.

The strangest thing, perhaps, is that the Castle Hotel does not have more ghosts. The building and its surrounding site, redolent with history and such horrific events as the mass hangings of the Bloody Assizes, could marshal a legion of spirits in many another place.

The phantom violins, it seems, manifest themselves only to discerning visitors. This is an hotel which could claim plenty of those.

[21] CLEARWELL CASTLE Heart of England

Clearwell, Royal Forest of Dean, Gloucester GL16 8LG
Telephone: 0594-832320
Fax: 0594-835523

Rooms: include 3 twin, 12 double
Location: Rural *Price Range:* ££
Restaurant: à la carte £-££; table d'hôte £
Facilities: Historic building; extensive grounds

Deep in an ancient royal hunting forest, in a landscape that has hardly changed over the centuries, Clearwell Castle was built in castellated style in the early eighteenth century. There has been a building on this spot for more than 900 years – it was the site of a Roman villa, and later a Crusader's manor house. An Elizabethan mansion belonging to statesman Sir Nicholas Throckmorton provided the basis for the present building, which was the home of the Wyndham family until the 1920s.

Now it is an elegant hotel. The huge Georgian reception hall, with its chandeliers and welcoming fires, also serves as a comfortable lounge. The warmly panelled dining room, where an excellent international menu is on offer, is a tribute to the restorations carried out in a very sympathetic style by the then owner, Colonel Vereker, in 1929 after an extensive fire which reduced the castle to a shell.

Today, the castle is still being restored by the Russell Steele family, whose flair for furnishings has made the hotel a very homely and comfortable place. Each of the 16 bedrooms has an historic bed: four-poster, half-tester, or just one with a magnificent headboard. And guests will find a bowl of fruit and a decanter of sherry in their bedroom to welcome them.

The castle and its grounds are sprawling, but are not so large that you feel lost. The castle itself is full of nooks and crannies, where chairs and coffee tables have often been cunningly placed to provide what amounts to a private sitting room. In the grounds there is stabling, while a large family of peacocks who think they own the place strut up to greet cars turning into the forecourt. Back inside, the sweeping staircase and vaulted banqueting hall can give the impression that time has stood still at Clearwell Castle – although the good service and 'mod cons' belie that.

The Forest of Dean is on the border between England and Wales, close to the beautiful Wye Valley. It is sporting country, with fishing, golf and horse-racing all nearby. But the area is so full of history that the castle's varied past blends in with the present and makes this a very pleasant place to visit. Sir Walter Raleigh thought so, and courted a daughter of the house; he would recognise the pillars in the banqueting hall, and other panelling though the castle's corridors, which date from Elizabethan times, but – sadly – his love affair ended up in the Tower of London. As then, Clearwell Castle is a nicer place to stay than the Tower. And, as an hotel, it represents excellent value for money.

THE GHOST is that of Sir Walter Raleigh's girl-friend, Bess, who committed suicide when Raleigh was banished to the Tower of London and she was ordered to marry someone else chosen by her father.

Although no-one has ever seen Bess, she is blamed for the inexplicable moving of furniture in one of the hotel bedrooms, 'The Boudoir', when the room is empty. In the same room, the wardrobe doors sometimes open of their own accord, and lights which are not connected to the main electrical circuit switch themselves on and off.

Another of the hotel bedrooms, 'The Vereker', is notable for its indefinable chill, despite excellent heating. One guest emerged pale, trembling and weeping – without being aware of the state he was in. Others have refused to remain in the room. The uncharitable might blame both on the room's odd shape and somewhat turbulent colour scheme.

Never mind: the hotel has a variety of other ghosts. The spectre of Lady Throckmorton, the wife of the owner, who died in the fire of 1729, has been seen walking up a staircase which is no longer there (the stairs were moved during the rebuilding). In 'The Baynham Room', which has two massively heavy half-tester beds, the beds have been found in the middle of the room, and the linen in an untidy heap, after the room was serviced – although no guests staying in the room have ever reported seeing or experiencing anything unusual.

One visitor who did refuse to remain in the hotel was a woman who said she had seen a group of Roman soldiers marching across the grass 'roundabout' in the middle of the hotel's forecourt. That was in 1990: a few months later the hotel's owners discovered that a Roman road ran under that very spot.

22 COMLONGON CASTLE — Lowlands

Clarencefield, Dumfries DG1 4NA, Scotland
Telephone: 038787-283
Fax: 038787-266

Rooms: include 5 double, 1 twin, 1 family room
Location: Rural   *Price Range:* £££
Restaurant: table d'hôte ££
Facilities: Historic building; extensive grounds

Surrounded by woodlands and apple orchards, an ancient feudal tower rises above the Solway Firth. A Borders stronghold built by Sir Cuthbert Murray in the fifteenth century, Comlongon Castle has walls 13ft thick, a chapel, the Great Hall and a master bedroom suite with a very 'mod con' for the 1400s – an en suite lavatory chute in the thick wall.

But you can't stay in it. It is the abutting Jacobean house which

Comlongon Castle

is now a comfortable hotel run by the Ptolomey family, and which has more up-to-date mod cons. From the moment the massive oak-bound door swings shut behind you, the house with its panelling, marble fireplaces and flagstones wraps its warm and welcoming atmosphere around you. The Ptolomeys have made an historic study of the Keep, and have filled the public rooms of the hotel with period items to enhance the atmosphere. That includes suits of armour, heraldic shields, battleaxes, fire-irons, and other regalia, some of them made to authentic patterns by Tony Ptolomey in his workshop. For besides running an hotel, Tony Ptolomey has a most unusual hobby: he makes suits of armour.

Comlongon Castle has just been refurbished, and has eight delightful, well-furnished and comfortable bedrooms, with four-poster beds. Some rooms have spa baths. The lounge has an elegant Adam ceiling, and its terrace overlooks the gardens and meadow sweeping down to a stream known as the 'Bonnie Burn'.

Home cooking is the keynote of the hotel's restaurant, in a Jacobean panelled room with a gleaming wooden floor. The Ptolomeys' table d'hote menus are excellent value – which is just as well, for guests are taken on a candlelit tour of the old Keep after dark by Tony Ptolomey and need sustaining. The tour is an amazingly atmospheric event, from dungeon to larder and on to lady's bedchamber. If you join the tour, look out for the mummified cats which Tony unearthed while restoring the Keep – they were put there to keep witches at bay.

Even in daylight, the peacocks which patrol the hotel's lawns can startle the unwary with their unearthly shriek. But for walkers and fishermen the grounds are a haven: a bridle path leads through the woods full of flowers and down to the Solway Firth.

Comlongon Castle is just a few miles from Robert Burns' burial place in Dumfries, and from Gretna Green. The hotel also makes a good jumping-off point for tours of the Galloway coast. And the hills of the Lake District are just across the water.

THE GHOST is that of pretty teenager Marion Carruthers, who more than 400 years ago defied her father when he wanted her to marry a neighbouring nobleman. Rather than obey, she jumped to her death.

High up in the forbidding walls of the old Keep there is a tiny window which overlooks the gardens and the stream. That narrow view was all that Marion saw for the six months her father kept her imprisoned for her disobedience. Kept on starvation rations in an attempt to bring her to her senses, Marion had plenty of time to consider her plight. But starvation strengthened her resolve to choose her own husband and when, in September 1564, her father gave her an ultimatum, she leapt from the narrow window to her death.

Tony and Brenda Ptolomey have met Marion. She walks through the gardens every year on the anniversary of her death – September 30 – wearing a green gown. Her appearance is heralded by a strong scent of apples. One theory is that Marion is seeking a Christian burial, for her vindictive father had her buried in unconsecrated ground somewhere in the woods behind the castle.

I was there on September 30, but the only scent of apples I could find came from Brenda Ptolomey's kitchen where dessert was in the making. But I did notice something odd: below the window of Marion's cell, among lush undergrowth and pretty garden flowers, on the spot where her body landed, nothing will grow.

Perhaps when Marion is resting safely in the churchyard, the Ptolomey's shrubbery will grow at last.

② CRAYKE CASTLE   Yorkshire & Humberside

Crayke, Yorkshire YO6 4TA
Telephone: 0347-22285

Rooms: 2 double, 1 twin
Location: Rural
Price Range: ££
Restaurant: en famille table d'hôte £
Facilities: Historic building

The all-powerful medieval Prince Bishops of Durham had lands extending far beyond the confines of Durham itself, and Crayke Castle was once a fortified palace in which the bishops and their followers maintained their presence among the unruly Yorkshire peasantry. Built in the fourteenth century, the castle is now a small hotel, its ancient face concealing the most modern and luxurious comforts.

Set square at the end of a sweeping drive, the castle has jagged battlements which remind guests of its original purpose. Inside, the owners have maintained the stonework nooks and crannies in their atmospheric home, while converting it to accommodate guests in an *en famille* style which shows off the hard work they have put into restoring the castle from its once appallingly neglected state.

The lounge has a huge arched stone fireplace, fit to roast a sheep, and there are roaring log fires in season. Dining is family style, but the standard of the five-course dinners is excellent and guests get a complimentary pre-dinner drink.

There are only three bedrooms, but they are equipped to a very high standard, with antique furniture and elegant drapes. Two rooms have four-poster beds, and they all have a warm and friendly atmosphere – not to mention fine views.

Crayke Castle is very well-placed as a touring base. The walled city of York, with its fine Minster, is only a short drive away, and the wild Yorkshire moors are all around – making the hotel a wonderful base for walkers and naturalists. Coastal resorts like Scarborough and Bridlington are within easy reach.

THE GHOST is more a wet patch than a wraith. There is a stubborn bloodstain on the floor near the wall between the kitchen and dining-room which resists all attempts to remove it. It fades, then reappears.

In Crayke Castle's six centuries of existence, it has seen its fair share of violence. There are tales of a Viking leader who was captured by the local peasantry whilst attempting a spot of rape and pillage and who met his death in a pit of writhing snakes.

But the phantom bloodstain is more likely to be associated with Crayke Castle's permanent house-guest: an unseen but genuinely tangible Spanish sea captain. Quite who he was, and what he was doing to suffer the fate that befell him, no-one is sure. But during the reign of Queen Elizabeth I, he arrived at Crayke, perhaps as a survivor of the ill-starred Spanish Armada wrecked on Britain's storm-lashed coast. And he is still there.

He was discovered during restoration work. While creating a hatch between kitchen and dining-room, the previous owners found his skeleton bricked up in the thickness of the wall. The hatch was moved elsewhere, and the sea captain's remains left undisturbed in their final resting place.

The captain has not been seen in corporeal form. But his presence is sometimes felt as a coldness – and there is that permanent and mysterious stain ....

24 THE CROWN HOTEL AND POSTING HOUSE
Yorkshire & Humberside

High Street, Bawtry, nr Doncaster, South Yorkshire DN10 6JW
Telephone: 0302-710341
Fax: 0302-711798

Rooms: include 15 double, 39 twin
Location: Central   *Price Range:* ££
Restaurant: à la carte ££; table d'hôte £
Facilities: Lift

The Crown Hotel, Bawtry

On the old main road to York, and a regular stop for the stage coaches of the eighteenth century, is the Crown Hotel at Bawtry. The old inn dates back well over 300 years, and among its former guests is the infamous highwayman, Dick Turpin. Perhaps he was there to plan one of his hold-ups or perhaps he merely needed a rest from his labours. Another traveller who enjoyed the comforts of the Crown was the writer Daniel Defoe, creator of Robinson Crusoe, in the early eighteenth century.

Today's visitors will find the Crown full of interesting period touches, which give a warm, comfortable, and perhaps timeless atmosphere, The oak-panelled Crown Bar offers a range of bar snacks throughout the day. The cocktail bar and Club House Restaurant are decorated in a bright nineteenth-century style, with brass chandeliers and quiet alcoves, and the menu has such traditional favourites as steak-and-kidney pie on offer as well as a wide range of international dishes.

The hotel's 57 bedrooms are prettily decorated, and have all modern amenities. And in the older part of the hotel there is a magnificent suite, furnished with elegant drapes and antiques, containing a four-poster bed.

The lovely cathedral cities of York and Lincoln are only an hour or so away by car, and the Yorkshire Dales and the Peak District of Derbyshire are a scenic excursion from Bawtry. Stately homes like Clumber Park, Thoresby Hall and Nostell Priory, designed by Robert Adam, are all nearby. Wragby Church, at Nostell Priory, contains a unique collection of Swiss painted glass. And if you fancy a flutter on the horses, the racecourses of York and Pontefract are both only a short drive away.

THE GHOST is one of a trio of spirits who make themselves known to staff and guests in the old part of the building.

Perhaps the oldest – in historical terms if not in actual age – is a monk who, in the early days of the inn's history, was accompanying his abbot back to their monastery high on the Yorkshire moors. The party stopped at the Crown for fresh horses and their journey must have been a long and tiring one for the monk, no longer in the first flush of youth, was trying to harness a horse when he collapsed and died of a heart attack. Now he is often seen in what was the old stables.

Prettier by far are the two female ghosts. One is a crinolined lady, her hair piled high in the fashion of the mid-eighteenth century, who floats amid her wide skirts along the upper corridors. It is thought she was a well-to-do traveller who perished in a fire caused by a carelessly snuffed candle.

The other is the ghost of a waitress. She dates from the early years of this century, when a waitress on the staff of the Crown was murdered by a jealous lover. Quite what sparked the quarrel and what happened to the murderer, is not clear. But the waitress, still apparently with plates in her hands, glides through the bars and kitchen areas of the hotel.

25 CULCREUCH CASTLE   Central Scotland

Fintry, Stirlingshire G63 0LW, Scotland
Telephone: 036086-228
Fax: 0532-390093

Culcreuch Castle

Rooms: include 5 double, 2 twin, 1 family room
Location: Rural   *Price Range:* ££
Restaurant: à la carte ££; table d'hôte £
Facilities: Historic building; golf; fishing; watersports; shooting; extensive grounds

Garden enthusiasts gather at Culcreuch Castle, near Stirling, to enjoy the 1600 acres of grounds, part of them wild, which border the River Endrick. The fells and woodlands around the two lochs within the estate offer endless walks, and sports like fishing and rough shooting are available. The castle's historic walled garden and pinetum, planted in 1842, are a treat at all seasons.

The castle itself is the oldest inhabited castle in central Scotland and was built in 1296 for the chief of Clan Galbraith. In Jacobean times it became the private home of the Barons of Culcreuch. Today the castle is a comfortable and unassuming hotel, which offers baronial banquets and other entertainments in such ceremonial rooms as the Laird's Chamber and the Galbraith Banqueting Hall. But as a guest in the castle, visitors may prefer the more intimate restaurant which offers a good table d'hote menu with a 'Taste of Scotland'.

The hotel's eight bedrooms are all furnished in antique style, with many baronial touches. Thick walls keep out the draughts, and some rooms have canopied half-tester beds with thick drapes. One room has hand-painted Chinese wallpaper.

The country park surrounding the castle has eight self-catering chalets hidden in secluded corners, for visitors who prefer a DIY holiday.

Culcreuch Castle's present owners have made the estate a friendly place to stay, away from the hurly-burly, but with plenty going on to keep visitors entertained. There is boating on the lochs and riding nearby. The cities of Glasgow and Edinburgh are both less than an hour away by car if visitors feel the need to desert the open fireplace of the Carved Hall or the elegance of the Picture Drawing Room.

Culcreuch Castle

THE GHOST in Culcreuch Castle is more of a happening: the wailing of pipes which is often heard in the dining-room and which seems to come from beneath the floor.

I stayed in the castle as the guest of a former owner, Baron Hercules Robinson, some years ago and, although the 'pipes' did not play the night I dined there, 'Herky' Robinson and his family had a strange tale to tell. They and other guests had thoroughly searched every nook and cranny of the castle and found no possible explanation for the sound – which they heard most nights during dinner. Wind whistling through the ancient stones? They thought so too. But, just out of interest, they recorded the sound.

They then took the tape to a very learned society in Edinburgh – and the musicologists there were fascinated. 'Where on earth,' they asked Herky, 'did you get this tape of ancient bagpipe music played on pipes without drones?' The drones, they helpfully pointed out, were added to bagpipes only after the Jacobite rebellion of 1745.

Culcreuch Castle has another oddity in the shape of a bedroom which is decorated with Oriental wallpaper and is known as the Chinese Bird Room. Some people say that the pipes are heard there too – but that was not Baron Robinson's story. What is certain is that the room has a very odd atmosphere, and of all the 'haunted hotel' bedrooms I have ever visited, the Chinese Room at Culcreuch is the only one I have refused to sleep in – although I could not attempt to explain why.

One Dutch visitor braver than I slept in the room and, before retiring, locked the door and set up his camera with the shutter open and a wide-angle lens covering the room. He closed the shutter before daylight and thought no more about it until he returned home and got the film developed.

The night-time photographs showed his shadowing figure asleep on the bed. Seated on the blanket box at the foot of the bed, however, was another figure – a vague white-clad shape. Who it was or is, nobody knows.

26 THE DOLPHIN HOTEL   South of England
High Street, Southampton, Hampshire SO9 2DS
Telephone: 0703-339955
Fax: 0703 333650

> *Rooms:* include 20 double, 16 twin, family rooms
> *Location:* Central *Price Range:* ££
> *Restaurant:* à la carte ££; table d'hôte £
> *Facilities:* Lift; gardens

Royal patronage has been part of the Dolphin's Hotel's history throughout the years, as seagoing monarchs spent the night here, and the double-fronted building with its bow windows still carries the coat-of-arms of King William IV and his Queen. They are not the only notables to have enjoyed the Dolphin's comforts: Queen Victoria stayed here; and authors Jane Austen and William Thackeray both visited the hotel during their travels.

There was an inn on this site in the thirteenth century, and the present hotel has Elizabethan features mixed in with the prevailing Georgian elegance. One of the public rooms, the County Room, has an ornate ceiling, and the lounge is panelled in warm wood with the odd nautical touch, reflecting Southampton's maritime heritage. The Nelson Bar continues the nautical theme.

The Thackeray Restaurant, where palms and mirrors lighten the pastel colour scheme, features standard international dishes and a buffet. The hotel's 73 bedrooms are all furnished in period style, with toning fabrics, and have every modern comfort. The Southampton Suite, with its own lounge, has views over the gardens where there are summer barbecues. The gardens are also a pleasant place to stroll with an after-dinner drink – an unexpected luxury in a city-centre hotel.

Southampton is not just a busy commercial centre, but has chunks of its history still on display. The fourteenth-century Bar Gate is an imposing edifice, and there is a fascinating maritime museum in the old Wool House. Even more historic Portsmouth, the Isle of Wight, the New Forest and the seaside resorts of the south coast are all within easy reach, making the Dolphin an excellent touring base.

THE GHOST is that of a cleaning woman at the hotel in the nineteenth century. She loved her work – so much that even today she can scarcely bear to leave it. She is often seen busying about her chores in the public rooms.

Molly, as she is affectionately known, is an early riser. Or perhaps she prefers night work, for she is usually to be found in the early hours of the morning, a floating shape which seems to be sweeping, or dusting. Night owl guests and night staff have often come across her. Unfortunately for the real cleaners, the results of her labours are as intangible as she is.

Molly's real name and identity are not clear. But, even allowing for the lateness of the hour at which she is usually spotted, she is accompanied by a clearly identifiable side-effect: a marked drop in temperature within a radius of several yards. Perhaps that explains why those who have seen Molly working up a sweat have felt a cold shiver down the spine.

27 DORMY HOUSE HOTEL   Heart of England

Willersley Hill, Broadway, Worcestershire WR12 7LF
Telephone: 0386-852711
Fax: 0386-858636

> *Rooms:* include 11 double, 25 twin, 2 suites
> *Location:* Rural   *Price Range:* ££££
> *Restaurant:* à la carte £££; table d'hôte ££

Walls of mellow Cotswold stone conceal a mellow heart in the Dormy House Hotel, set on its hilltop just outside the beautiful village of Broadway. A seventeenth-century farmhouse, it has been carefully extended and converted in harmony with its setting. The buildings now house a luxury hotel with more than its fair share of nooks and crannies for dining, enjoying a drink, or just plain sitting. Log fires and exposed beams, flowers, and contemporary prints and paintings preserve the rural atmosphere of the original farm without any of the modern amenities being neglected.

The owner, Ingrid Philip-Sorensen, oversees everything with

Dormy House Hotel

great personal flair, and the comfort and charm of the busy hotel is a tribute to her skills. Despite its conference facilities, which are in a separate annexe, the hotel is a haven of peace, and staff have that magical knack of knowing a guest's name from the first moment. The restaurant, formed from a series of the original farmhouse rooms, is stone-walled and very cosy and intimate. An exceedingly high standard of international cuisine is presented by the Dormy House's award-winning chefs.

The bedrooms all differ in style, according to their size, shape and location. Chintzes and flower prints echo the old-world charm of the rooms, and there are handsome carved beds and four-posters. Some of the rooms open on to their own walled gardens, which are ablaze with English cottage-garden flowers in season. And all the rooms have the modern touches of TV, direct-dial telephone and other facilities, all planned to sit in with the farm-house character that this efficient hotel preserves.

Antique-hunters will enjoy Broadway, noted for its curio shops, and the nearby Cotswold villages of Bourton-on-the-Water, Burford, Chipping Campden and Evesham. Stratford-upon-Avon is only 15 miles away, and for the outdoor enthusiast there is golf, riding, and many interesting rambles in the gentle hills. Who knows, there may even be the chance of finding a cache of Roman silver – as happened recently near the Dormy House. Both the Romans and the ancient Celts loved this area and seemed reluctant to leave – a feeling which guests at Dormy House may share.

THE GHOST is that of a little old lady who – unusually – seems to have moved into one of the newer parts of the hotel. The bar of the conference suite is built over part of an Iron Age settlement, and when the foundations were being dug for the extension to the hotel the excavators unearthed bones and burial urns. But the old lady does not appear to date back as far as the Iron Age. She has floating grey garments, and looks rather poor. But she has found a nice little niche for herself in an armchair – dating from the eighteenth century – which stands, oddly solitary, against the back wall of the bar area.

Nobody has hazarded any guesses as to who she might be, but she does seem to be a sociable soul who enjoys a crowd and a spot of music. Her appearances are erratic, but have always coincided with a party or similarly lively function in the conference suite.

Many guests have noticed the old lady sitting in 'her' tapestry chair, looking very much like one of the group. Some have approached her to strike up a conversation – but as they drew near she simply evaporated.

With such a high-profile ghost in the newer part of the hotel, it is almost a disappointment to find that the older parts of the seventeenth-century hotel have little to offer in the way of spectral encounters.

But walk along the passageway to bedroom 6 and you will encounter, almost outside the door, the most clearly defined 'cold spot' that I have ever experienced. The icy chill covers an area not more than a footstep across, but is so noticeable that you consciously look around for a cause.

Your search is in vain. The windows are all tightly shut, and the central heating is hissing happily to itself. But some people have reported odd goings-on in Room 6 which does just happen to have an old four-poster bed. Another old lady has allegedly been seen there, and when she leaves the room she does so in style: she disappears through the wall into the adjoining Room 5.

28 THE DUKE'S HEAD   East Anglia

Tuesday Market Place, King's Lynn, Norfolk PE30 1JS
Telephone: 0553-774996
Fax: 0553-763556

> *Rooms:* include 31 double, 14 twin
> *Location:* Central   *Price Range:* ££
> *Restaurant:* à la carte ££, table d'hôte £
> *Facilities:* Lift

This imposing pink-washed building in classical style faces proudly on to King's Lynn's main market square, known as the Tuesday Market Place. The hotel was built as a tribute to the area's agricultural and textile affluence, and has presided over many dealings

The Duke's Head

between the region's farmers and merchants over its 300 years of existence.

Inside, the hotel has maintained an air of Georgian elegance. Reception is slick and efficient, and the lounges and bars are decorated in pastel colours to show off the plasterwork and panelling. The restaurant is rather more Victorian in style, and its menu – of which the hotel is justly proud – combines the best of local ingredients with international dishes. The portions should satisfy the heartiest appetite and the range of home-made desserts is tempting.

The hotel has 65 bedrooms, all recently refurbished and decorated to a high international standard and offering all modern amenities. The rooms have a variety of pretty and harmonising colour schemes with matching drapes and spreads to suit each type of room.

King's Lynn has a wide range of historic buildings, from the fifteenth-century Guildhall of St George, once a theatre, to the seventeenth-century Custom House, down on the quay, which was designed by the same architect as the Duke's Head. Many of the town's medieval houses have been restored, and there are some fascinating memorials in the town's churches.

The royal residence of Sandringham is only a few miles away, and the long sandy beaches of North Norfolk's coast are within easy reach. There is a wide range of wildlife in the area, and stately homes include Holkham Hall and Blickling, the childhood home of Anne Boleyn.

THE GHOST is that of a maidservant who was executed in the square outside the hotel during the eighteenth century. She is seen in the corridors as a misty shape, moving with a stealthy motion.

There are many reports of this ghost, but no-one has yet managed to identify her despite her public execution. Local stories abound concerning the events that took place on hanging days in the huge square. In those days women were liable for the death penalty for minor crimes by today's standards, and many died on the gallows outside the Duke's Head. So she may have been only a minor miscreant. But the favoured story is that the maidservant decided to do away with her mistress while they were staying at the hotel. Somehow she got hold of a deadly poison, and administered this to her mistress, who died in agony.

Whether the maid's motive was greed, robbery, or revenge for some real or imagined slight, is not recorded. But the girl was executed for her crime in front of a rowdy crowd of local people. Since then, she has been seen by staff and guests moving through the upper corridors of the hotel. I have not seen her, but I am told that she looks singularly unrepentant.

29 DUNKENHALGH HOTEL — North West

Clayton-le-Moors, nr Blackburn, Lancashire, BB5 5JP
Telephone: 0254-398021
Fax: 0254-872230

Rooms: include 33 double, 31 twin, 10 family rooms
Location: Rural   *Price Range:* ££££
Restaurant: à la carte only ££
Facilities: Historic building; leisure club; snooker; extensive grounds

Dunkenhalgh Hotel

Separated from the urban sprawls of Blackburn and Bolton by lovely upland country, the Dunkenhalgh (pronounced 'Duckenhash') Hotel is an elegant mansion recently converted and restored to its former glory and now a comfortable and historic country house hotel.

First logged in local records in 1285, the estate has passed through many hands, the house being extended and rebuilt rather haphazardly, until an eighteenth-century owner took his courage in both hands and rebuilt the old hall in classical style. It now features a castellated roofline, with turrets at various points.

Overlooking 17 acres of part, the present house has many lovely public rooms used for meetings or private dining, including the exquisite Portrait Room with ormolu-framed family portraits set in the plasterwork panels. The Oak Room is panelled in dark, rich wood, and dates from the house's earlier days. The Cameo lounge and bar have a fresh-air feel, due to their setting in a walled courtyard which has been glassed over and filled with plants and greenery.

The Cameo Restaurant is a shell-pink oasis where meals are served in an unhurried atmosphere, and where the menus have a range of such traditional favourites as steak-and-kidney pie alongside international dishes. Weekend guests will find that there are dinner-dances on Fridays and Saturdays, with the hotel's resident singer to entertain them.

The 80 bedrooms are well furnished, spacious, and have every modern comfort alongside their period decor and chintzy colour schemes. A range of in-house movies is available on television for night-owls. If livelier entertainment is needed, there is the Dunk Inn, the hotel's own pub, in the converted stables – a spot also popular with locals. Its low arched ceilings and alcoves make it an atmospheric place for an evening's live jazz or disco – or even a friendly sing-song. The hotel also has its own leisure club with a swimming pool, snooker tables and health treatments.

There is a lot to see and do in the area: Manchester with its museums and galleries is nearby, and there is much in the way of industrial heritage in Bradford and Halifax.

THE GHOST is that of Lucette, a governess to the Walmsley family who owned the mansion in the eighteenth century.

Lucette made the mistake of falling in love with one of the sons of the household, who was promptly packed off on a European 'grand tour' in the hope that he would forget his infatuation with someone that the family saw as 'beneath him'. Broken-hearted, Lucette drowned herself in a lake in the grounds.

Today, a misty figure is still seen walking down the corridors, leaving the hotel, and taking the path towards the lake. The hotel's public relations representative says that sightings are quite frequent, and that the figure is sad rather than frightening.

30 DWELDAPILTON HALL HOTEL
Yorkshire & Humberside

Appleton-le-Moors, North Yorkshire YO6 6TF
Telephone: 07515-227
Fax: 07515-540

Rooms: include 5 double, 6 twin
Price Range: ££
Facilities: Gardens
Location: Rural
Restaurant: table d'hôte £

For once, the Post Office got it right. When the nineteenth-century mailmen met to decide on the postal name for the pretty Yorkshire village where Dweldapilton Hall is the most important building (if you don't count the church and the pub), they settled on the charming name of Appleton-le-Moors.

In the *Domesday Book* the village was called Dweldapilton, after the Hall. But the present Hall is not so ancient: it was built in the earlier years of Queen Victoria's reign and is now a comfortable country house hotel.

The building is of local stone with a pillared entrance porch rising to the second floor. Inside, there is a cosy bar with wood panelling, a comfortable lounge, and an attractive dining-room decorated with an eye for period detail beneath ornate Italian plasterwork ceilings. The Dweldapilton dining experience is as English as its setting among the Yorkshire hills: the table d'hote menu changes daily but features classic British dishes with a home-cooked flavour, imaginatively prepared by owner Brenda Smalley. And there are log fires to relax beside after dinner as you sample the hotel's speciality – a range of malt whiskies.

The 12 bedrooms are all carefully decorated to reflect their ambience, with carved beds and attractive soft furnishings.

There are lovely views from the terrace, which is a pleasant spot for afternoon tea in summer. The two acres of gardens are full of bright flower beds and specimen trees.

The village itself has a lot to offer. Off the beaten track, it has somehow missed being catapulted into the twentieth century and its main street retains much of its past charm. There is even a restored medieval mill to visit, and the lovely unspoilt countryside all around.

The medieval city of York, with its minster and 'Shambles' of cobbled streets, is only a short drive away. The spa town of Harrogate, the racing centre of Thirsk, and the seaside resorts of Bridlington and elegant Scarborough all make interesting excursions.

THE GHOST is that of the original owner of the house, who built it in the 1860s with money made as a slave trader. He died in a riding accident, but appears whenever new owners are making changes to 'his' house.

It seems he is just curious. And perhaps just a little resentful. New owners were always suffering from a rash of minor accidents. The present owners went through this: china would smash without apparent cause; they would suffer minor falls and odd illnesses. Then their mother, whose room was in the old part of the house, disclosed that on the back stairs leading to the kitchen she had often passed the elegant figure of a handsome man wearing a tall Victorian stove-pipe hat.

Taking her courage in both hands, Brenda Smalley sat on the stairs one night and 'told him off'. Since then his behaviour has improved – but he is still seen in the house, keeping an eye on proceedings.

31 EASTWELL MANOR   South East England

Eastwell Park, Boughton Aluph, nr Ashford, Kent TN25 4HR
Telephone: 0233-635751
Fax: 0233-635530

Rooms: 20 double, 3 twin
Location: Rural   *Price Range:* £££££
Restaurant: à la carte ££; table d'hôte ££
Facilities: Historic building; tennis; croquet; snooker; extensive grounds

An eleventh-century manor house was the first home to be built on this site and its successor is a mock-Tudor building erected from original materials in the 1920s. All the houses were named after a spring in the area known to Saxon herders and there are other age-old connections. In the fifteenth century, Eastwell Manor harboured an illegitimate son of King Richard III, and when he was discovered by a follower of the new Tudor dynasty he was allowed to remain nearby, living out his days in a humble cottage near the manor.

A tenant in Victorian times was the Queen's second son, Prince Alfred. But for many of the house's 900 years it was safely in the hands of the prolific Finch family: in King Charles II's time one Finch patriarch produced 27 children.

Today Eastwell Manor is a lovely grey stone house rebuilt entirely from the stone of earlier houses. The 1920s owner, the flamboyantly-named Sir John de Fonblanque Pennefather, added a variety of European bits and pieces to the house: Italian ceilings, French panelling and other treasures collected on his travels. The end result is unexpectedly charming and is now the Eastwell Manor country house hotel.

The house has open fires with massive carved overmantels, intricate plasterwork ceilings, and much panelling and leather furniture to enhance the club-like atmosphere. The dining-room is an elegant room, and serves the best of 'English Fayre' alongside a selection of French dishes.

At the top of the oak staircase carved with gargoyles and family crests, are the 23 bedrooms – all vast and airy, elegant and distinguished. Named for former owners, many of the rooms have their own sitting areas, and all have the modern amenities expected of such a luxurious hotel. The Middleton Suite has a vast Edwardian marble bathroom. Furnishings are sumptuous and include lovely antiques.

The hotel has 62 acres of grounds, containing mature trees from all over the world. There is a lake, stocked with fish, and beautiful formal gardens. Tennis and croquet are available; and for less clement days there is a snooker table indoors.

The town of Ashford is nearby, with good shopping. Dover, with its maritime and wartime connections, is an interesting excursion and the historic towns of Hastings, Rye and Winchelsea are delightful to visit.

THE GHOST is a White Lady, sometimes seen at the top of the stairs.

Her attire has made some people think that she might be a Cistercian nun: there was a Cistercian foundation nearby in medieval times, and because superfluous daughters were often packed off to nunneries against their will to get them out of the way, the theory is that she could be a member of the original Eastwell family suffering from a 700-year-old bout of homesickness.

But an alternative theory is that she is a dowager Lady Finch, from Charles I's time, who was a secret Roundhead sympathiser despite her Royalist upbringing. 'White Lady' spirits are supposed to be idealists, so one must suppose that she is mourning the eventual loss of the Puritan cause as Cromwellian principles crumbled to make way for Charles II.

32 ELVEY FARM   South East England

Pluckley, near Ashford, Kent TB27 0SU
Telephone: 023384-0442

Rooms: include 3 double, 2 twin, 5 family rooms
Location: Rural   *Price Range:* £
Restaurant: en famille table d'hôte £

Elvey Farm

This is a family farm which has used its old oast-house and other outbuildings to provide holiday accommodation with a difference. Elvey Farm lies in the heart of the orchards of Kent, and has been in the present owners' family for many generations. The lovely old buildings have been well maintained and have a delightfully rustic air without the real farmyard intruding.

Guest bedrooms are spacious, and have been furnished with great care and eye to detail. There are oak beams everywhere. Some of the rooms in the sixteenth-century oast house are completely circular. There are family rooms, in the former stables, and all guest accommodation has well-stocked refrigerators.

Dinners are family-style: hearty fare cooked with flair. But if guests prefer they can cater for themselves in a separate kitchen – a boon for anyone with faddy children or in need of a special diet.

Pluckley, which has the reputation of being England's most haunted village, is near Ashford, and the lovely city of Canterbury with its magnificent cathedral makes an interesting excursion. Dover is within easy reach, as are the seaside resorts of Hastings, Margate and Ramsgate. In short: a great place for a family holiday.

THE GHOST is that of Old Bill, a farmworker who died about 100 years ago. He is often seen in one of the rooms in the old oast-house, sitting on the end of the bed. Perhaps this is the room that Bill used when he worked at the farm.

The Harris family, in whose ownership the farm has been for generations, have often seen him, and visitors have been known to wake up in the night in one of the oast house guest rooms to find Old Bill sitting in his shirt-sleeves and chatting to unseen companions.

He is glad of the company, it seems, and spends hours sitting at the foot of the bed. Some guests have seen him, gone to sleep again, and re-awakened to find him still there – and still gossiping. He is clearly visible, and almost tangible. But he cannot be heard, so his night-time chats need not be disturbing.

The Harris's have an archive of old family photographs, and will show anyone interested a snapshot in which Old Bill appears, wearing a collarless shirt and looking just as he does in his ghostly form. So if you wake up to find a venerable yokel at the foot of your bed, at least you'll know whose room you are sharing.

33 ETTINGTON PARK HOTEL

Heart of England

Alderminster, nr Stratford-upon-Avon, Warwickshire CV37 8BS
Telephone: 0789-450123
Fax: 0789-87472

Rooms: 39 double, 9 twin, including 9 suites
Location: Rural   *Price Range:* £££££
Restaurant: à la carte £££; table d'hôte ££
Facilities: Historic building; lifts; leisure centre; fishing; riding; tennis; gardens; extensive grounds

A grand baronial chateau set in an estate which has been in the same family since the Domesday Book is now one of England's finest and most discreet hotels. The Shirley family farmed at Ettington Park even earlier than the Norman Conquest, and have built a succession of imposing houses on their lands. The present house, which combines parts of the mansions of the fourteenth century and other eras, dates principally from the late 1700s, and has been turned into an hotel which is a visual delight.

Set beside the River Stour, the neo-Gothic mansion reveals an interior in the grand manner of the Victorian country house. A palm-filled conservatory leads into the hall with sweeping carved staircase. The great drawing-room is a sunny retreat for a quiet drink over the morning papers, and its adjoining book-lined library is now the hotel's bar.

Filled with antiques and original paintings and old prints, the house has very atmospheric corners – like the medieval chapel, now used as a private dining room, and the Long Gallery, created to house the family's heirlooms. The dining room is set under an ornate rococo ceiling, and there are hand-carved family crests set into the panelling. The menu reflects the Victorian opulence of the house with some of the most imaginative dishes to be found in any country house hotel.

Each bedroom has been furnished in a distinct style to reflect its particular character. Some are on two levels, with twisty stairs between, and there are four-poster beds and lavish drapes paired with tasteful pictures and objets d'art to create a comfortable and welcoming ambience.

The estate contains a wealth of sports facilities for visitors, from fishing in a private stretch of the River Stour to horse-riding and all-weather tennis courts. There is a swimming pool in the leisure centre, which is part of the main hotel building.

This is Shakespeare country, of course. His birthplace in Stratford is just six miles away, and visitors should not miss seeing Ann Hathaway's cottage at nearby Shottery. His plays are performed in repertoire throughout the year at the Royal Shakespeare Company's Stratford Memorial Theatre. Birmingham and Coventry, with its beautiful modern cathedral, are within easy reach. And the Cotswolds are on the doorstep.

THE GHOST is not really a ghost, more a regular but inexplicable occurrence. An old book in the library, which is now the hotel bar, has a habit of defying those who are trying to keep it in its place on the shelves. No matter how tightly it is jammed in among its fellows, it regularly falls to the floor at midnight.

And it always falls open at the same page – a page containing a quotation from Wordsworth's poem 'St Ronan's Well'. The verse warns grimly: 'This place is cursed'.

Guests need not be afraid; the warning is aimed at members of the Shirley family, who still own the building, and the book falls only when a member of the family is in the house – although that is quite often.

Staff regularly find the book lying open on the floor, and have kept vigil to see it fall. Weird, they say, but not scary. For guests, the book's movements have been known to provide an excuse for raiding the brandy bottle – even if they did deplete the stock of gin-and-tonic while awaiting the event.

The Shirleys are not a lucky family. Various tragedies are associated with them. In the nineteenth century one unfortunate daughter of the family hanged herself from the chandelier over the staircase, and her grey, wraithlike figure is sometimes reported to have been seen revolving slowly over the stairwell.

The Long Gallery of the hotel is similarly spooky; it resounds to the sound of running feet even when it is locked and empty. The sound, some say, is of servants hurrying to rescue the twin children of the family who drowned in the river running through the grounds. And many people staying in the Tower Suite have awakened to the sound of children crying – even though there are none in the house.

34 THE FALMOUTH HOTEL — West Country

Castle Beach, Falmouth, Cornwall TR11 4NZ
Telephone: 0326-312671
Fax: 0326-319533

Rooms: include 9 double, 36 twin, 12 family rooms
Location: Central but peaceful   *Price Range:* £££
Restaurant: à la carte ££; table d'hôte £
Facilities: Leisure centre, snooker, outdoor swimming pool; croquet, putting; gardens

The Falmouth Hotel

Falmouth is dominated by the Victorian bulk of the Falmouth Hotel. Its broad frontage overlooks its own promenade gardens and the sea, with an endless succession of ships passing to and fro in one of the world's greatest natural harbours.

Purpose-built in the 1860s, the Falmouth Hotel still has an air of Victorian opulence. The entrance hall has a lofty ceiling with elegant chandeliers, and the pretty Camellia Lounge opposite the reception desk was originally the Ladies' Parlour.

The public rooms are all elegantly and comfortably furnished. The bar and restaurant have panoramic views and are pleasant places to relax. The restaurant serves delicious meals, with English favourites enjoying a fresh and imaginative touch.

The hotel's 73 bedrooms all have sea-views, and some have grand balconies. They are all comfortably furnished, and there is a refurbishment programme well under way. The bridal suite has a pretty pink four-poster bed, and there are several rooms with whirlpool spa baths. All the bedrooms have the usual modern amenities, and all are spacious and attractive.

But for all its Victoriana, the Falmouth Hotel is not lagging behind the times. A brand-new and very attractive leisure centre with health treatments and an indoor swimming pool has opened recently, and the five acres of gardens boast an outdoor pool, a croquet lawn and a putting green. The beautiful and mature gardens are full of exotic palms and pretty shrubs and a walled kitchen garden supplies the annual seedlings as well as many of the fresh vegetables used in the kitchen.

The Cornish coast, with its romantic bays and coves, extends for many miles around the pretty town of Falmouth, and there are many fascinating villages to explore – especially around the banks of the river Fal. Cornwall is a garden county, and there is what is supposed to be the most beautiful churchyard in the country at St Just, in the Roseland peninsula, as well as four of England's loveliest gardens – Trelissick, Trebah, Glendurgan and Penjerrick – which are all worth visiting. Nearby, too, is the Lizard Peninsula, the romantic and ancient St Michael's Mount and, of course, Land's End.

THE GHOST is that of a brewery worker who haunts what is now the snooker room of the hotel.

When the hotel was built, in Victorian times, it used to brew its own beer in one of the myriad of cavernous rooms in the basement. Two brewers manned this enterprise, and one of them unexpectedly collapsed and died whilst working amid the barrels.

As customs changed, the rooms 'below stairs' gradually became nothing more than store-rooms which were seldom entered by staff, let alone guests. But with the recent development of a health and leisure club in the hotel, many of the rooms have been opened up again, cleared out, redecorated, and pressed into service as recreational facilities. The old brewery is now the Snooker Room.

But the old brewer is still there, if staff are to be believed. Health club manageress Joanne James has felt him watching her when she has been vacuuming the room late at night, and her young assistant, Mark, won't go in there at all at night since he felt a strange vibration whenever he stood at one particular spot.

The room does have an atmosphere, but that could be explained by its musty smell and specialist lighting. But Joanne says: 'I feel that whoever is there means no harm. He's quite friendly really'.

35 THE FINNYGOOK INN   West Country

Crafthole, Cornwall
Telephone: 0503-30338

The Finnygook Inn

Rooms: 3 double, 1 twin
Location: Central but quiet   *Price Range:* £
Restaurant: à la carte £; table d'hôte £
Facilities: Gardens

A pretty pink inn on the rock coast of Cornwall in the village of Crafthole, the Finnygook Inn was established in the early years of the sixteenth century. It became very popular with villagers and fishermen, and today it is just as popular – both with locals and with visitors to this lovely corner of England.

What the inn was called originally has long been forgotten, for the name it bears today recalls a daring smuggler in the 1700s called Finny. The low, beamed bar of the inn was his headquarters, and the beams today bear a quotation appropriate to Finny and his exploits: 'There is a tide in the affairs of men, which, taken at the flood, leads on to fortune. Omitted, all the voyage of their life is bound in shallows and in misery'. It is Shakespeare, from *Julius Caesar*.

Guests following Finny's footsteps (but hopefully not his career) find a comfortable and convivial atmosphere in 'his' bar, and an excellent restaurant which serves good English cooking. The restaurant is in a newer part of the building, and has its own lounge and bar furnished in a bright modern style.

The inn has four comfortable guests rooms, all well if simply furnished, and with all modern conveniences. Owners Roger and Janet Wiseman enjoy making guests feel at home, and will even serve breakfast in guests' rooms.

The Finnygook Inn is on the shore of Whitsand Bay, not far from Torpoint and the city of Plymouth. There are the lovely coves and beaches of the Cornish coast all around, while inland lie the mysterious moors and a lot of glitzy theme park-style attractions. There is sailing and birdwatching, and golf on the nearby Whitsand course. For excursions, the pretty towns of the region – Fowey, Truro, Helston, and Padstow with its Mayday 'Obby 'Oss parade – are all within easy reach.

THE GHOST is that of Finny, the smuggler who used the bar of the inn as his headquarters. 'Gook', incidentally, is the Cornish word for ghost – hence the inn's name.

Finny was not just a smuggler, he was also a wrecker – luring ships to their doom on the rocky south Cornish coast in stormy weather by waving lamps on the shore. When merchant ships hit the rocks, their crews would be murdered and the goods on board would be carried off by Finny and his men to their secret storerooms in the tunnels beneath the Finnygook Inn.

But Finny met a well-deserved death when one of the tunnels collapsed whilst he was inside gloating over his ill-gotten gains, somewhere around 300 years ago. He suffocated in the earth and dust.

However, he is still to be seen on occasion propping up the bar of the pub to which he gave his name. Visitors and locals alike report a misty figure, bearded and recognisably dressed in seafaring garb and high boots, standing just below the beam bearing the inscription from *Julius Caesar*. When people approach the figure, it vanishes.

36 FORDE ABBEY West Country

Chard, Somerset TA20 4LU
Telephone: 0460 20231

Rooms: 8 double
Location: Rural
Price Range: £££££ (inclusive of meals and drinks)
Restaurant: en famille haute cuisine
Facilities: Historic building; extensive grounds

An *en famille* experience in the grand manner is on offer at Forde Abbey, in Somerset. A stately home of the very stateliest kind, it was once a twelfth-century Cistercian abbey. Now it is the home of Mark and Elizabeth Roper, who enjoy sharing its grandeur with guests on a house-party basis.

The surroundings are immensely elegant. The present house incorporates the original abbey buildings, which were converted to family use in 1649 by Sir Edmund Prideaux whose taste for the classical style blended remarkably well with the last abbot's efforts in the perpendicular style. The house is vast, lake-girt and set in 25 acres of impeccable grounds; it is also open to the public, and is full of treasures and objets d'art accumulated by careful owners over the centuries.

The Saloon, which is rather too grand for comfortable sitting, houses one of the nation's great treasures: the Mortlake Tapestries, woven especially to fit this room from the cartoons by Raphael which are on view in the Victoria and Albert Museum.

Dining is a more intimate experience than that enjoyed by past owners, who sat in the Great Hall at the High Table. And the dishes served today are in the best English grand style.

The house has eight guest bedrooms, five of which have en suite bathrooms, and there is always the chance that you will be allocated the Grand State bedroom. To give the real house-party feeling in these magnificent surroundings, the Ropers prefer parties of six or more to come along together, perhaps just to enjoy grand family living or perhaps for a private shoot on the estate in season.

For all the grandeur of the surroundings, the Ropers make visitors feel very much at home. The many lounges and studies offer a wealth of intimate corners for relaxing in with pre-dinner drinks or morning coffee – all of which come as part of the experience.

Chard itself is a delightful town, famous for its lace-making, and, less peacefully, for Judge Jeffreys and his Bloody Assizes in the eighteenth century. Bath is nearby, and the Somerset countryside is fun to explore.

THE GHOST is that of a monk, one of the original Cistercian friars who lived in the Abbey until its transformation to a private house in 1649. He regularly takes his place at the High Table in the Great Hall for meals.

It is said that he is seen in many areas of the house associated with food – and that he was perhaps responsible in his lifetime for provisioning the Abbey. Undaunted by the classical music concerts and recording sessions that happen in the Great Hall on some 100 days a year, he has been seen as a rounded, brownish shape sitting stolidly at the High Table as if waiting to be served.

But times have changed. Gone are the spare meals of his monastic days; gone, too, are the lavish feasts and classical banquets of the seventeenth and eighteenth centuries. And even the Victoria opulence and large family gatherings have changed. Now dining is on a much more intimate scale at Forde Abbey.

Perhaps the hungry monk is losing heart, for he has been seen less and less frequently of late.

37 GAIRNSHIEL LODGE Tayside & Grampian

Glengairn, Ballater, Aberdeenshire AB3 5QU, Scotland
Telephone: 03397-55582

Rooms: include 2 double, 1 twin, 4 family rooms
Location: Rural *Price Range:* £
Restaurant: family style table d'hôte £

It is not a grand hotel by any means, but if you like good home-cooked meals and a family atmosphere then try this small hotel not far from the royal holiday home of Balmoral Castle. Gairnshiel Lodge, once a royal hunting lodge, is now an hotel run by Martin and Monica Debraemaker, who specialise in home cooking and (in

Martin's case) home brewing. Together they make the drive up Glen Gairn worthwhile.

Gairnshiel Lodge stands beside the River Gairn above Ballater, in the foothills of the Cairngorms, and is a paradise for walkers, birdwatchers, skiers and lovers of the Highlands. The granite house, set in its four acres of grounds, is an ideal family holiday spot, once enjoyed by Queen Victoria's children who spent their summers there.

Homely comfort is on offer, with a pleasant dining room, an upstairs sitting room with a log fire, and shelves of books and board games to choose from. There are beautiful views over the glen to the mountains, especially at sunset.

The lodge's bedrooms are all sizeable, and some have en suite facilities. All are warmly and comfortably furnished. There is a games room, and displays of local crafts to tempt the souvenir-hunter. The only drawback to the hotel is its popularity – so many visitors have fallen under its spell that they come back year after year, and anyone wanting a room there in the summer needs to book well in advance.

Ballater, where every other shop is 'By Royal Appointment', is only six miles away and Braemar, where the famous clan 'Gathering' is held on the first Saturday in September, is close by. So there is plenty to do in the area – although this is really a nature-lover's and sporting centre, with regular sightings of buzzards, deer, pine martens and wild cats in the glen.

THE GHOST is not just a single spectre, but an entire ghostly army. This modest but extremely homely and comfortable hotel overlooks a beautiful packhorse bridge which, for centuries, has been the only way across the River Gairn on the road between Glenshee and Royal Deeside. And many people staying at the hotel have reported hearing the tramp of an army crossing the bridge in the middle of the night.

The sound is unmistakeable. Besides marching feet and the jingle of horses' hooves, witnesses have heard the rattle of cannon being dragged over the humpbacked centre of the bridge. But people who have dragged themselves reluctantly out of bed to see what all the noise was about have found the bridge, and indeed the entire glen, totally deserted.

Local residents are unamazed by the phenomenon, which they say has been going on for centuries and is the sound of General Wade's army marching across the Highlands during their task of putting down the clans after the Jacobite Rebellion of 1745. According to them, this is one of the most widely observed (or perhaps one should say heard) ghostly occurrences in Scotland.

The Debraemakers, on the other hand, insist that their slumbers have never been disturbed – and neither were their predecessors. If you are interested, Rooms number 5, 7, and 9 overlook the bridge. If you would rather be told about it next morning, then the other guest rooms look safely up the glen.

Because they haven't heard the ghostly army themselves, it would be easy to dismiss the owners as unimaginative sceptics. Unfair! They may not entirely believe in Wade's soldiers, but it is hard not to believe in the ghostly old lady who a young visitor saw smiling down benignly from the first-floor landing. The child described the woman to the previous owners and they passed on the description to the postman. He immediately identified her as the late former owner.

And one of the hotel's maids refused to service Room 3 because an unseen cat kept brushing against the back of her legs when she was making the beds. The Debraemakers don't keep a cat.

38 THE GEORGE HOTEL — South East England

High Street, Crawley, Sussex RH10 1BS
Telephone: 0293-524215
Fax: 0293-548565

> *Rooms:* include 26 double, 29 twin, 15 family rooms
> *Location:* Central   *Price Range:* £££
> *Restaurant:* à la carte £; table d'hôte £
> *Facilities:* Lift

It is amazing how well one can sleep under the shadow of the gallows. At the George, that is a commonplace experience – for the

The George Hotel

old inn, in the centre of the bustling town of Crawley, near Gatwick Airport, has an ancient gallows as its sign, stretching right across the High Street.

Dating back to the sixteenth century or earlier, this is an old coaching inn. The vast carved fireplace in the hall bears the date 1615, and the timbered walls and beams give a very traditional atmosphere. The lounge and bars are cosy, and there are leaded windows with attractive stained glass designs. The Kings Restaurant serves meals as elegant as the decor of the room in which they are eaten, the woodwork and later Georgian panelling adding to the warmly hospitable atmosphere.

The 86 bedrooms are all furnished to an international standard, and amenities include tea and coffee-making facilities. The family rooms are generously proportioned, and the rooms in the older part of the hotel have some historic touches.

Although it is in the town centre, the hotel is generally peaceful – but a wide range of function rooms make it a busy place on occasions. However, the staff are never too hurried to make guests feel at home.

Apart from being convenient for Gatwick Airport, to which the hotel's courtesy bus runs regularly, the George has the rolling North Downs on its doorstep, with superb walking on the ridge from Box Hill to Reigate Hill. Crawley has many leisure facilities and both London and the South Coast are less than an hour away by car, coach or train.

THE GHOST is that of Mark Hueston, nightwatchman of the inn in the eighteenth century. He had a taste for wine, especially at others' expense, and this proved his undoing.

The inn had a problem with a persistent thief, who was stealing guests' valuables from their rooms. Mark was told to look out for intruders, and sat up all night in the broom cupboard in the corridor to keep an eye on things. But the then owner did not know that Mark had a habit of popping into the guest rooms himself for a nip or two of the wine from the bedside decanters.

During the night, Mark duly refreshed himself – so thoroughly that he fell into a drunken sleep in his broom cupboard and missed another series of robberies. The irate owner found both jewels and wine missing, and gave Mark one more chance to catch the thief. But he also set a trap of his own. Unfortunately, on his next vigil, Mark again fell prey to the lure of free wine. He drained another decanter, retreated to his broom cupboard – and died there. For the owner, convinced that wine thief and jewel thief were one and the same, had filled the wine jugs with poison.

Was Mark the guilty party? No-one knows. But he still keeps watch in the corridors, where he has often been seen by staff and guests. And 'his' broom cupboard, outside Room 7, is often found open after the housekeepers have shut and locked it. The bedroom doors in the hotel's old wing often open and close noisily and of their own accord when nobody is nearby – so perhaps Mark is protesting his innocence. Or perhaps he is searching for a glass or two of wine.

39 THE GLOBE HOTEL   West Country

Fore Street, Topsham, nr Exeter, Devon
Telephone: 0392-873471

Rooms: include 4 double, 5 twin, 3 family rooms
Location: Central
Restaurant: à la carte £
Price Range: £
Facilities: Historic building

At the heart of the picturesque port of Topsham, the 400-year-old Globe was once a popular and successful stagecoaching inn on the Exeter to London run. Today it still caters for the needs of travellers in its new role as a comfortable and very atmospheric small hotel on the estuary of the River Exe.

Run by a relative newcomer to Topsham, Mrs June Price, and her family, the Globe has many features that its visitors from the 1700s would still recognise. The vast Devon-style inglenook fireplace in the bar, for example, with its salt cupboard and arch above the massive lintel niches; or the big bow windows; and especially the warm welcome. The bar is dim and cosy, and very popular with locals and visitors alike. The restaurant, with log fire, serves a range of good standard dishes, with a homely touch and good-sized portions. Reserving a table is advisable, as Mrs Price's cooking is justly popular; but the restaurant is closed on Sundays.

The hotel now has 14 bedrooms, most in newly and imaginatively converted outbuildings belonging to the original inn, including an old Malt House, which ring the courtyard. In the main building the bedrooms are furnished simply but comfortably, with historic beds, including a four-poster bed and a massively carved half-tester bed. The four-poster room has arched double doors, with a knocker and a strange peephole secured inside by a bolted shutter – relics from the days when it was Topsham's masonic headquarters. All the bedrooms have modern amenities.

Topsham, once one of Britain's major ports but now a quiet holiday town, is only 10 minutes' drive from the city of Exeter, with its good shopping and attractive historic remains. The river is within sight of the Globe, and there is fishing, boating and excellent walking all along the estuary.

Visitors should take time to explore the glorious Devon countryside, with its cottage-made clotted cream teas tempting them at every turn. The wildness of Dartmoor is within easy reach, and pretty villages nestle among the woods and combes. Plymouth and Dartmouth, with their naval heritage, are also worth a visit.

THE GHOST is an unseen 'presence' felt by many guests as they walk across the steeply sloping floor of the landing outside Room 5. But owner Mrs June Price has never heard or seen anything.

However, a much more tangible 'something' was dug up when workmen were excavating around the old inn courtyard as part of the preparations for new guest accommodation. They found a jumble of bones, buried in quicklime.

Topsham was agog. They hadn't seen anything like it since the Armada. The town's policeman was called in and, presumably because he was the only other uniformed official around, the town's traffic warden was called in too.

Everyone was secretly just a little disappointed when scientists pronounced the bones to be 400 years old. And, far from being human, they were those of a large dog.

Room 10 now stands over the canine crypt and Mrs Price, who

is not without a sense of humour, has hung a picture of an alsatian in the room and delights in asking guests whether they have been disturbed by a spectral hound of the sort more usually connected with nearby Dartmoor.

A few guests have been caught, but most spot the joke. But the joke may yet be on Mrs Price because, although no present member of staff has seen anything, the locals who gather in the bar every night are quite convinced that the Globe is haunted by whatever it is that walks the upstairs corridor – and has been for centuries. In such an atmospheric building, full of unexpected nooks and crannies, it is hard to ignore these local tales.

40 THE GOLDEN LION — East Anglia

Market Hill, St Ives, Huntingdon, Cambridgeshire PE17 4AL
Telephone: 0480-492100

Rooms: include 8 double, 2 twin, 3 family rooms
Location: Central *Price Range:* ££
Restaurant: à la carte £

Next to the church and the market square in the little town of St Ives, on the edge of the Fens, the Golden Lion is an old coaching inn dating back to the Middle Ages. It now boasts a smart white Georgian facade, and its main entrance is the broad arch through which coaches used to pass on their way to the stableyard.

Inside the family-owned hotel there is a comfortable bar, enjoyed by the locals, and a restaurant in which an everyday menu offers a good choice of food and excellent value for money in homely surroundings. The 21 bedrooms, carefully modernised to provide good basic comforts, mostly have pretty pastel colour schemes and en suite facilities. There are large rooms which can take a family of four with ease, and even the single rooms are comfortably sized.

Upstairs, a pleasant long gallery serves as a lounge, and the bedrooms lead off it. The floorboards are part of the older inn, and it is not difficult to imagine Oliver Cromwell striding along the gallery issuing orders right and left – as he must surely have done when he made the inn his headquarters during the Civil Wars. The gallery overlooks the courtyard and although the first-floor balcony is now glassed in, it still has its pretty Georgian wrought-iron balustrades.

St Ives is a good shopping centre and the River Ouse, which runs through the town, is ideal for boating, fishing, or just strolling beside. The town's market day, on Monday, is a bustling affair, and if the shops pall there is a large sports centre and a golf course nearby. Peterborough, Huntingdon and Cambridge are all within easy reach, and one of the few remaining estate-villages in the country, colourful Abbots Ripton, is worth a visit.

THE GHOST is that of Oliver Cromwell, who commandeered the inn for use as his headquarters during his Civil War campaigns in the region and whose statue stands in the street outside the hotel. He has been seen in one of the bedrooms – albeit infrequently.

Seen slightly more often is a female ghost, the Green Lady, known familiarly to hotel staff and regularly as 'Ivy'. Ivy is thought to have been nursemaid to Oliver Cromwell's children, and – despite his espousal of Puritan ethics – Cromwell's mistress too. She is said to have hanged herself in Room 13.

Tracking her down is difficult because the bedrooms were not numbered in the days when the Golden Lion was a coaching inn, and even today there isn't a Room 13. The only clue is that the room in which she died is known to have had oak beams. Several of the bedrooms have such beams.

The hotel receptionist, a down-to-earth Scots lass, who has worked there for 12 years, has never seen the Green Lady. Or Cromwell either, come to that.

But if you want to know what the Green Lady looks like, you have only to dine in the hotel's restaurant. A rather fanciful likeness of her hangs over the fireplace: she is dressed in a classical-style green dress and wears a headdress of ivy leaves which doubtless explains her nickname.

The picture of 'Ivy' will never be a great work of art. But it does have a peculiar quality in that the Green Lady's eyes seem to follow you around the restaurant – and her expression changes as you move. In most parts of the room she looks benign and even innocent. But in certain lights, as you walk towards the door of the restaurant, her expression becomes baleful and her eyes flash angrily.

If she looked like that at Oliver Cromwell, the man who was called the Lord Protector of England might have felt in need of a bit of protection himself.

41 THE GRAND HOTEL   East Midlands

St Mary's Street, Lincoln, Lincolnshire LN5 7EP
Telephone: 0522-524211

> *Rooms:* include 19 double, 13 twin, 1 family room
> *Location:* Central   *Price Range:* ££
> *Restaurant:* à la carte £; table d'hôte £ Abbey Grill Room (coffee shop style) £
> *Facilities:* Lift, business services

A row of Georgian houses in the centre of the beautiful old cathedral city of Lincoln has been converted into a comfortable and welcoming hotel: the Grand. Its long white facade might seem more at home in a seaside resort, but the hotel has a business-like heart and is extremely popular with the local people.

Warm velvets and natural woods are the decorative themes throughout the hotel, and the lounge and two bars have a pleasant ambience. The West Bar offers not only drinks but a range of bar meals, and the Tudor cocktail bar makes a cosy spot for a pre-dinner drink. The main restaurant, with very good value dishes from a classic menu of tried favourites, has an excellent reputation. There is a coffee-shop, the Abbey Grill Room, which serves lighter meals and grills all day.

The hotel's 50 bedrooms are simply but comfortably furnished, although some of them are mysteriously equipped with three-quarter-sized beds. Amenities include double-glazing, essential in a city-centre hotel, and the hotel's business facilities include a range of meeting rooms and commercial services.

Lincoln is dominated by its magnificent cathedral, high on a hill above the narrow streets. There are street markets, museums, excellent shopping, and a Roman port at Brayford Pool. The city, on the edge of the Fens, is surrounded by flower and vegetable-growing areas, and the sites of many of the Second World War airfields. York, King's Lynn and Stamford are among the historic cities within easy reach.

THE GHOST is that of Bobby Broadbent, once the owner of an hotel which now forms part of the Grand. He bought a row of cottages in the 1920s and turned them into a pair of hotels: letting one and running the other himself. But, not long after the work was completed, Bobby died suddenly – and he has since often been seen in the attics of the 'rival' hotel which was highly successful while Bobby's own half of the building languished.

He seems to be jealous of the success of the other hotel, and his spirit has been blamed for a number of mishaps during the life of the Grand, which was converted into one hotel under independent ownership in the 1950s.

The Grand's manager, Neville Rose, who has been with the hotel for many years, was so convinced that the shadowy figure of Bobby was responsible for odd happenings there that he and other members of staff held seances in the afflicted attics – with 'spectacular results', says Neville. Bobby has now become a peaceful inmate, and his interference in the daily running of the hotel has ceased. But he is still seen occasionally.

The seances revealed other intangible guests at the Grand: there is an old lady who is often seen in Room 27, and either she or another spirit seems to enjoy disturbing the slumbers of guests in the neighbouring Room 29: as recently as Easter 1990, proprietress Carole Wootton reports, a young woman guest refused to stay in the room after her bed was shaken and dragged across the room while the wardrobe doors were rapidly opened and closed by unseen hands.

42 THE GROSVENOR HOTEL

South of England

The Commons, Shaftesbury, Dorset SP7 8JA
Telephone: 0747-52282
Fax: 0747-54755

Rooms: include 12 double, 12 twin, 4 family rooms
Location: Central   *Price Range:* ££
Restaurant: à la carte ££; table d'hôte £

An old coaching inn, with a history going back more than 400 years, lies behind the elegantly colonnaded Georgian exterior of the Grosvenor hotel. Situated right on Shaftesbury's Market Place, the hotel still has a wide coaching gateway which nowadays leads to a pretty patio garden in the heart of the building.

The hotel has been carefully modernised in keeping with its Georgian appearance, and the main rooms are elegantly furnished and bright with rich drapes at the tall windows. The lounge on the first floor has a display of antiques including one quite famous treasure: a vast, ornately carved, oak sideboard known as the Chevy Chase sideboard. The Grosvenor Hotel need not fear for the safety of this particular piece of furniture – it would take a small army to steal it!

The Huntings Bar, which overlooks the patio garden, has many pleasant corners filled with paintings, and in summer the bar area is extended to include the patio, where cream teas and other refreshments are also served.

There's a Georgian atmosphere again in the Grosvenor Restaurant, where the menu's emphasis is on traditional English cuisine. The cellar contains a noteworthy range of port wine.

The hotel's 35 bedrooms are mostly furnished in comfortable international style, and the family rooms are especially spacious. Two bedrooms feature antique four-poster beds, and these have a particularly rich colour scheme and soft furnishings. All the bedrooms have modern conveniences.

Shaftesbury is at the heart of 'Thomas Hardy Country', amid

scenery and places featured in his novels. Shaftesbury itself has one of the most picturesque streets in the country: Gold Hill, with its steep cobblestones and pretty stone cottages. Nearby are the lovely house and gardens at Stourhead, the stately home of Longleat with its lion park, and the Fleet Air Arm Museum at Yeovilton.

THE GHOST is a thirsty one, with a taste for beer rather than... er... spirits. No matter how carefully beer stocks are checked, and the cellar doors locked, beer regularly and unaccountably goes missing: the levels in the barrels on tap dropping with no human agency or leakage to account for it.

Staff blame the misty figures of monks, who are seen regularly in the passages beneath the hotel in the area around the cellar. They seem to be monks of the merry kind, like Friar Tuck, and date back to the days when a medieval monastery was nearby and the passages were used by the monks going to and from their devotions.

Besides the beer-swilling monks downstairs, the Grosvenor is graced upstairs by a charming apparition known as the Grey Lady. Who she is, and why she walks the bedroom corridors in the older parts of the building, is not known. She has often been seen by guests and staff near the huge Chevy Chase sideboard in the upstairs lounge: so perhaps she is a former owner of the piece – or perhaps just an admirer of the massively fanciful item of furniture.

43 THE HAYCOCK HOTEL East Anglia

Wansford-in-England, Peterborough, Cambridgeshire PE8 6JA
Telephone: 0780-782223
Fax: 0780-783031

Rooms: include 36 double, 8 twin
Location: Adjacent to the A1, but peaceful   *Price Range:* £££
Restaurant: à la carte ££; table d'hôte £; bars (buffet) £
Facilities: Historic building; business centre; boule; cricket; gardens

The Haycock Hotel

A seventeenth-century coaching inn still survives today as one of the prettiest and most rambling hotel buildings in the country. In its time the Haycock Hotel has been a farm, a hunting box, a racing stables and even an ammunition factory during the First World War. Happily, the maze of buildings has grown up around the old inn's courtyard – and the result today is an extremely imaginatively restored range of mellow buildings housing bars and sitting-out corners at every turn.

There are comfortable lounges, and the pretty walled gardens lead down to the River Nene – which has been known to invade the old inn in the days before flood controls became more efficient.

Plenty of good food is on offer in the hotel's restaurants: traditional English cooking to complement the hotel's own heritage, using fresh ingredients from the surrounding Fens. The 51 bedrooms come as a happy surprise: comfortable and well-equipped, of course, but the soft furnishings have all been selected to suit the room and have been chosen with a real eye for effect. What do the rooms you don't see look like? The answer can be found in the hotel's vast 'quilt' hanging on a staircase wall, in which pieces of all the cloths used in the refurbishment have been used to make a colourful collage. Some of the bedrooms themselves have oak beams, others have four-poster beds. And a series of new rooms has been built in keeping with the old parts of the hotel, and these open on to the walled gardens.

Mary, Queen of Scots, stayed here en route to her imprisonment at Fotheringhay nearby, and Queen Victoria, before becoming Queen, slept in the Gainsborough Room.

The hotel stands in six acres of grounds, and offers a boule court, its own cricket field, and of course the rushing River Nene. It was the river which gave both the hotel and the village their unusual names. An early patron of the inn, 'Drunken Barnaby', dozed off on a bale of hay after his midday imbibings – and awoke to find the Nene had flooded and that he was floating downstream on his hay raft. He panicked and called to onlookers to know where he was. 'Wansford', they said. 'Wansford-in-England?' the stupefied man yelled back – and the village has been Wansford-in-England ever since.

Peterborough, with its Norman cathedral and excellent shopping, is some ten miles away. And Lincoln and the Fenlands are within easy reach for a touring holiday.

THE GHOST is more a very strange atmosphere, apparent in some of the hotel's otherwise warm and welcoming bedrooms. If you are allocated one of the single rooms numbered 202, 204 or 207, and are a trifle over-imaginative, you might do well to move to another room.

Over-imaginative? One of the hotel's night porters, a very levelheaded and down-to-earth man, found himself very reluctant to go along the corridor outside these rooms. And one night, when he had his sheepdog with him for company, the dog refused pointblank to turn the corner into that passageway. Such behaviour was unusual for the dog, so the porter toured the hotel with it and approached the same passageway from a different direction. Once again, the dog would not turn the corner.

There is another room, a two-tiered room, number 103, with dark oak beams and a high window, in which some guests have reported feeling cold and faint. But the management are glad to report that this is a rare occurrence, and it must be remembered that the hotel is an ancient and rambling building where the imagination does run riot.

But have the people who have seen a sad face, peering down into the hotel's courtyard from a high attic window, imagined it? It has been seen by staff and guests, who all describe the face as very forlorn.

I have been in the room from which the sad face peers. It is only a space under the rafters, full of the lumber of ages, and there is no access to it except through a tiny, very firmly locked, trap-door in a landing wall. There is nobody there, and no practical joker could get in there without dismantling a large chunk of wall.

Imagination again? Perhaps. But the night porter's sheepdog won't go near the trapdoor, either.

⁴⁴ HINTLESHAM HALL

East Anglia

Hintlesham, Suffolk IP8 3NS
Telephone: 047387-334
Fax: 047387-463

Rooms: 31 double, 2 twin
Location: Rural
Restaurant: prix fixe menu ££
Price Range: ££££
Facilities: Historic building; sports facilities; extensive grounds

Hintlesham Hall is not what it appears to be. Its elegant stucco exterior is that of an imposing Georgian residence – an impression underlined by the fact that it stands in an elegant park amid typically English countryside. But beneath the stucco is the original, timbered Tudor house, built in the 1570s for Thomas Timperley, grandson of the third Duke of Norfolk.

Far from having a split personality, however, the house's occupants over the centuries have managed to blend the Tudor and Georgian in a most attractive way. There is a largely Elizabethan rear-view over the park and stretches of water, while the elegant colonnaded entrance hall leads to lofty public rooms. Ornate plasterwork ceilings and pine panelling add grace to the rooms, and the book-filled library is a cosy retreat.

Hintlesham Hall

As befits a building first open to the public as a restaurant under master-chef Robert Carrier, the hotel is world-famous for its cuisine. Local specialities share the menu with international haute cuisine, and many of the ingredients and herbs are produced in the hotel's gardens.

Some of the hotel's 33 bedrooms are very grand; some just cosy. All are fitted and furnished to a high standard, and are very attractive. Four-poster beds and canopied beds predominate, and there is every luxury from bathrobes to mini-bars, with teletext TVs to hand.

Current owners Ruth and David Watson have brought their own taste in decoration and antiques to add to the already elegant and imposing building, and have taken up the sporting challenge by setting aside some of the estate's 175 acres for a championship-length golf course. And that's in addition to the snooker, clay-pigeon shooting, trout fishing, tennis and riding already on offer to visitors to the Hall.

If you can tear yourself away from all these activities, the international horse-racing and horse-breeding centre of Newmarket is nearby, and the beautiful Suffolk countryside immortalised by artist John Constable is on the doorstep. The seaside town of Aldeburgh, famous for its music festival, is another of the attractions within an hour's drive of Hintlesham.

THE GHOST is a very odd one: the waxwork model of a child.

In Georgian times, the twice-married owner of the house had to go away and left his beloved small daughter in the care of her stepmother. When he returned he was horrified to find the child – who the stepmother hated – starving, unkempt, and close to death.

The child died in his arms. And her distraught father dreamt up a gruesome revenge on his second wife. He had a wax model of the child made, depicting her as emaciated and prematurely aged. This he placed in a glass case on the landing.

Eventually, of course, the waxwork was destroyed. But in the 1890s, historian H M Vaughan – who did not know the story of the child – was visiting the then-empty house, and pulled aside some velvet curtains on the landing. 'What', he asked his guide, 'is that model of a child in the glass case?'

The guide hurried to his side and peered into the recess behind the curtains. It was quite empty.

45 THE KNIGHTS HILL HOTEL

East Anglia

Knights Hill Village, South Wootton, King's Lynn, Norfolk PE30 3HQ
Telephone: 0553-675566
Fax: 0553-675568

> *Rooms:* include 36 double, 12 twin
> *Location:* Rural
> *Restaurant:* à la carte ££
> *Facilities:* sports and leisure centre
> *Price Range:* ££

Staying on a farm takes on a whole new meaning at the Knights Hill Hotel, near the lovely Norfolk town of King's Lynn: for it once was a large farm. Now the hotel is part of a complex known as the Knights Hill Village, which has a range of leisure and meeting facilities carefully concealed among the original range of massive stone barns and outbuildings.

Under the sharply pitched and beamed roofs, the hotel's reception areas and public rooms are decorated in a country style with many rural antiques and interesting prints on the massively-cut carrstone walls. There are open fires with hefty oak lintels, and iron chandeliers to enhance the medieval atmosphere.

There is a country-pub style bar which serves light meals, and a formal restaurant where English and international favourites blend on the menu which is excellent value. Real ales also feature in the bars.

The 58 bedrooms are light, bright and modern, some on the ground floor opening on to a patio courtyard, and all have every modern amenity. There is a luxurious Master suite, as well as two rooms featuring four-poster beds and two with canopied beds. All the bedrooms are very comfortably furnished in period style, but with a touch or two of luxury.

The 'village' has many sports facilities – including a large new leisure centre with a swimming pool. There is tennis available, and a games room features snooker and other indoor sports.

But, for all the on-the-spot attractions, it would be a pity not to visit some of the lovely places in north Norfolk. King's Lynn itself is a blend of medieval and Georgian buildings, and the flourishing port comes complete with elegant eighteenth-century Customs House. The royal residence of Sandringham is only a short drive away, and the lovely beaches and wildlife preserves of the Norfolk coast make interesting and enjoyable days out.

THE GHOST is that of a farm worker, and is thought to date from Jacobean times when the hotel buildings were at the centre of a flourishing agricultural estate.

Guests sleeping in Room 5, which is over the kitchen, have often awoken to find a figure, dressed in simple rustic clothes, standing at the foot of the bed. But the appearance does not seem to worry guests too much because such incidents are merely reported, matter-of-factly, to the reception staff next morning.

46 LARKFIELD PRIORY HOTEL

South East England

London Road, Larkfield, Maidstone, Kent ME60 6JH
Telephone: 0732-846858
Fax: 0732-846786

> *Rooms:* include 11 double, 19 twin
> *Location:* Suburban but peaceful   *Price Range:* £££
> *Restaurant:* à la carte ££; table d'hôte £

Larkfield Priory Hotel, just a short drive from the busy Kent town of Maidstone, is one of those country house hotels which – rather like Topsy – have 'just growed' from a mixture of buildings and extensions. These range from the original house, several hundred years old, to the crisp new wing. But for all that, it has a happy atmosphere and the blend of old and new styles means that most visitors feel very much at home.

Victorian-style conservatories have been added to give space and sitting-out places. The hotel's restaurant, the Club House, is housed partly in such a conservatory overlooking the lawns, and is bright and fresh with lots of plants and greenery. The adjoining Club House lounge bar is a cosy place to sit and relax, and the large lawns make for pleasant strolling on summer evenings, while the bar's open fires are a great attraction in the cooler months.

The 54 spacious bedrooms are decorated in pretty chintzy style and have every amenity. In the older part of the hotel there is an attractive four-poster-bedded room, with light flowery drapes and pink toned decor.

Kent, rightfully known as the 'Garden of England' is a beautiful county of forests, narrow lanes, and historic cities. The latter include Rochester, Chatham, Canterbury with its beautiful cathedral, and Maidstone itself. Larkfield Hotel makes an excellent base for touring the region.

THE GHOST is that of Charlotte, who appears to hate kitchen chores. She has been seen in the old part of the house, which was built on lands which were once the property of the Archbishop of Canterbury, and she is thought to have been a servant in an earlier house on the site.

Staff and regular guests are used to greeting her familiarly by her nickname – which she doesn't seem to mind – as she glides along the corridors, her footsteps echoing belatedly behind her.

Recently, her footsteps took a turn from her usual route, and were heard descending the back stairs to a kitchen long since closed up for the night and, as usual, left in apple-pie order by the kitchen staff and chefs. When the staff reported for work next morning, they were amazed to open the kitchen door and find all the pots, pans, dishes and dry ingredients strewn over the floor, and all the taps turned on.

Charlotte has never misbehaved in such a way before, and at the time of writing this remains an isolated occurrence.

⁴⁷ THE LEARMONTH HOTEL

Central Scotland

18-20 Learmonth Terrace, Edinburgh EH4 1PW, Scotland
Telephone: 031-343-2671
Fax: 031-315-2232

Rooms: 12 double, 50 twin
Location: Central   *Price Range:* £££
Restaurant: à la carte ££; table d'hôte £
Facilities: Lift

In the middle of one of Edinburgh's lovely terraces of Georgian houses is a stately double-fronted building that is now the Learmonth Hotel. Only a mile from the historic centre of Scotland's capital, the Learmonth is remarkably peaceful, and is sheltered from the city traffic by the tree-lined terrace with its wide grassy verge.

Inside, the Learmonth has been carefully converted to offer a comfortable, business-like base for visitors to the city. There is a lively bar, Polly's Continental Cocktail Lounge, which offers a range of light meals throughout the day and is decorated in an interesting and rather art-deco style.

The hotel's main restaurant is a relaxed place to dine, in the cosy surroundings of pine panelling and cane-webbed chairs. The dishes range from tried and tested international favourites to classic Scottish specialities: haggis is generally available if you feel the need. The Fettes Suite is decorated is Scottish baronial style and in summer is the venue for 'Gibby's Ceilidh', a regular evening of Scottish folklore and food.

The 62 bedrooms are comfortably furnished in an international style, with every modern amenity. One has a four-poster bed. All are attractively furnished in pastel shades, making the rooms both bright and restful.

Edinburgh is a wonderful place for visitors, with its castle, old town, museums and art galleries, fine shopping, and of course the world-famous Festival each summer. The Forth Bridge, just over 100 years old, is a stunning sight with its atmospheric floodlighting. Glasgow, with its inspiring Burrell Collection of fine arts, is only an hour's drive away.

THE GHOST is a poltergeist who seems intent on ensuring that the night porter earns his keep!

Several holders of this nocturnal post have shut and locked doors only to find them standing open a few minutes later, while the sound of footsteps and whistling comes from a conference room which, upon investigation, is always empty. On one occasion recently, after these sounds had been heard, the conference room's fire doors swung slowly open as if moved by unseen hands.

Guests are undisturbed by these goings-on except that, in some bedrooms, the electric hair-driers have a habit of turning themselves on and off when the mood takes them.

48 LEE WOOD HOTEL East Midlands

The Park, Buxton, Derbyshire SK17 6TQ
Telephone: 0298-23002
Fax: 0298-23228

> *Rooms:* include 16 double, 11 twin, 2 family rooms
> *Location:* Central but peaceful   *Price Range:* ££
> *Restaurant:* à la carte ££; table d'hôte £
> *Facilities:* Lift; gardens

Sparkling spa waters and grand opera are on hand for visitors to the Lee Wood Hotel in the charming town of Buxton, set high in the Peak District National Park.

A late Georgian house, on one of Buxton's many hills, has been made into a very comfortable hotel by the Millican family, who have a very 'hands-on' approach to running their hotel, one of the oldest established in the town. Set in lovely landscaped gardens overlooking Buxton's park, and just a few minutes' walk from the town centre, the hotel has a conservatory restaurant which carries on the 'outdoors-indoors' feeling with views over the rooftops to the cupola of the Opera House itself.

The Lee Wood's lounge and cocktail bar are a pleasant place to relax before or after a meal in the conservatory, where good use is made of fresh, seasonal ingredients for the generous helpings. The hotel's bedrooms are bright and comfortable, in a style which echoes the period of the building, and have such modern amenities as trouser-presses, direct-dial telephones and hair-driers.

There is a second bar beneath the hotel: the Sherwood Bar. It is open in the evenings and offers a range of beers and traditional pub games – making it popular with the locals.

Buxton itself has a wealth of museums and galleries, and antique and speciality shops. It really comes to life during the annual arts festival in late July and August. On the doorstep are the peaks, caverns and stately homes of Derbyshire, and neighbouring towns like Matlock with its Heights of Abraham cable car and Gulliver's Kingdom theme park make the area a good base for family holidays.

There is a spa water swimming pool in Buxton, and the bottled water itself is, of course, beside your hotel bed. It is also piped into the fountain in the town centre for all-comers to sample. The sparkling variety is said to be good for rheumatism but, like many mineral waters, it is rather an acquired taste.

THE GHOST is of a woman in a billowing white gown, whose identity and connection with the building are both unknown.

A couple of years ago, a guest in Room 4 awoke to see the woman in white walking past the end of the bed. He thought it was his wife going to the bathroom – but then he noticed that she was still snuggled down beside him and fast asleep. As he tried to wake her to show her the mysterious apparition, the woman in white vanished.

The sighting was a solitary one, which makes co-proprietor John Millican slightly dubious about its authenticity. So guests with an inquiring disposition are particularly welcome in Room 4.

49 LEIGH PARK HOTEL West Country
Leigh Road West, Bradford-on-Avon, Wiltshire BA15 2RA
Telephone: 02216-4885
Fax: 02216-2315

Rooms: include 8 double, 5 twin
Location: Suburban   *Price Range:* ££
Restaurant: prix fixe menu £
Facilities: Tennis; snooker; croquet; extensive grounds

This gracious mansion is older than it looks. Leigh Park was originally an Elizabethan house, given by Queen Elizabeth I to her favourite, Robert Dudley, Earl of Leicester, in 1574. The Virgin Queen stayed here at that time, and enjoyed her stay so much that she was very reluctant to leave.

Hopefully guests are still reluctant to leave, for the present house – a Georgian building which includes some of the Elizabethan house – is now a very comfortable hotel owned by Peter and Carolyn Nannestad. Many of the original features are preserved in the present building, a handsome mansion with a pillared entrance portico.

The lounge, known as the Dudley Room, is homely, with deep velvet sofas and masses of flowers, and the restaurant has many period details. Much of the fruit and vegetables featured by the latter are grown in the hotel's walled kitchen garden, and accompany the traditional English and French cuisine which makes up the prix fixe menu. The restaurant has superb views over the Wiltshire Downs, and on a clear day one of the white horses cut into the chalk can be seen, although it is more than ten miles away.

The Winston Bar is named after a local dog, who deserted its owner and attached itself to the hotel's gate on a crossroads. It is a pleasant place in which to relax. Both the Winston Bar and the Dudley Room have a patio with views over the gardens towards Bradford-on-Avon.

There are 22 bedrooms, all delightfully furnished in the same timeless and elegant style as the public rooms. They are spacious and comfortable, and have all modern amenities. One has a charming lightweight Georgian mahogany four-poster bed.

Tennis, snooker and croquet are available at the hotel, and its five acres of grounds are lovely to stroll in. Bradford-on-Avon is a delightful and historic town with a rare bridge chapel, and Bath with its Roman remains and elegant shopping is only 15 miles away. Cheddar Gorge makes an interesting excursion, and the prehistoric sites of Avebury and Stonehenge are within easy reach.

THE GHOST is that of Robert Dudley, Earl of Leicester, who was Queen Elizabeth I's lover. She gave him Leigh Park 'for services for the state'.

The earl was something of a ladies' man – although the not-so-virginal Virgin Queen does not seem to have worried about that. Indeed, some historians believe that she loved him so much that he very nearly became king, and just possibly murdered his young wife Amy Robsart in order to do so. But he died in 1588, before any such union could take place. Now randy Robert haunts Leigh Park – but only female guests arouse his interest.

There are many reports of women who are staying at the hotel waking in the night to feel an 'extremely friendly' presence in their rooms, and feeling that someone is leaning over their bed. In every instance, the guest has said she felt as though she was being flirted with. Hubbies snoring beside their spouses do not put off the amorous earl – but no male guest has ever reported the ghost's presence.

Which room do you avoid if you don't fancy a spot of phantom flirting? Your guess is as good as mine – for the ghost's presence has been felt all over the hotel.

50 THE LORD CREWE ARMS

Northumbria

Blanchland, nr Consett, County Durham
Telephone: 0434-675251
Fax: 0434-675337

The Lord Crewe Arms

Rooms: 12 double, 6 twin
Location: Rural
Restaurant: prix fixe menus £
Facilities: Historic building; gardens
Price Range: £££

This warm stone manor house has stood on the same spot for more than six centuries, and only in the 1720s did it become a commercial inn. Earlier it had been part of the monastery in the village of Blanchland, under the Prince Bishops of Durham. So the hotel's traditions of hospitality go back as far as its foundations.

The building is much as it was in the mid-eighteenth century, and the main lounge is in the glorious stone-walled Hilyard Room with its huge arched fireplace, large enough to take a sofa and chairs and make a private sitting-corner. The Crypt Bar has low arched ceilings which recall its former life as a part of the old monastery, but the restaurant, which serves a range of prix fixe menus featuring local specialities as well as international favourites, is a more modern room and is pleasantly decorated in an up-to-date style.

The hotel has 18 bedrooms, some in a modern wing and pleasantly furnished with all comforts and many period touches. Those in the older part of the house have antique four-poster beds and half-tester beds, and are richly furnished in period style. Each room is individually decorated to suit its ambience, and there is a profusion of oak beams and mullioned windows to keep up the sense of being part of history that pervades the house. There is a bowl of fruit and a decanter of sherry in each room to welcome new arrivals.

There are lovely gardens around the hotel for guests to enjoy, and the village of Blanchland is only a short drive from the city of Durham with its massive castle and cathedral. The lovely beaches of Northumberland are nearby, too, and there is horse-racing at Hexham if you fancy a bet.

THE GHOST is that of Dorothy Forster, an eighteenth-century relative of Lord Crewe. The family were all Jacobite sympathisers, and Dorothy, still regarded as a heroine of the revolt, avoided arrest and helped her brother escape to France.

She is often seen in the Bamburgh bedroom of the house.

Dorothy's uncle by marriage, Lord Crewe, was well-known as a Jacobite sympathiser during the uprising of 1715, and as a Prince Bishop of Durham he had considerable sway among local inhabitants. Dorothy's brother, Tom, was something of a hot-head and got himself into a scrape which resulted in the house – then a hunting lodge in which Tom and Dorothy lived on their uncle's charity – being searched by the English troops.

Dorothy kept her head, and hid Tom in a secret chamber up the broad chimney of the massive fireplace in what is now known as the Hilyard Room. The soldiers failed to find him, and departed empty-handed. Dorothy arranged for Tom to flee to France where, some years later, he was murdered – probably by secret agents of the Crown.

Dorothy never saw her beloved brother again, despite trying to get messages to him that it was safe to return home. She died still missing him, and her spirit walks sadly in the room she frequented so much in her lifetime – the Bamburgh bedroom. She is seen only as a soft, hazy shape.

Recently, guests in other bedrooms in the old part of the hotel have reported waking in the middle of the night to find the dim shape of a monk kneeling by their bedside in an attitude of prayer. Quite why he should be praying beside beds that were not in existence when he was alive is a mystery.

51 LUMLEY CASTLE Northumbria

Chester-le-Street, County Durham DH3 4NX
Telephone: 091-389-1111
Fax: 091-387-1437

Rooms: include 36 double, 14 twin, 2 family rooms
Location: Suburban but tranquil   *Price Range:* £££
Restaurant: The Black Knight (international cuisine) à la carte ££; table d'hôte £; The Baron's Hall (Elizabethan feasts) £
Facilities: Historic building; lift; indoor swimming pool; extensive grounds

Lumley Castle

A medieval masterpiece built by Sir Ralph Lumley in 1392, Lumley Castle stands on a hillside high above the market town of Chester-le-Street, in County Durham. A fantastic crenellated stronghold originating in the ninth century, the castle is just as fantastic inside. It is now a highly individual hotel, and the property of a businessman who prefers to remain anonymous.

Whoever he is, he has great flair and imagination. He has done much of the design himself, and has taken all the awkward corners and shapes of the rambling old building and turned them to advantage in terms of space and decorative themes. One bedroom, for example, seems to have no bathroom until you open the doors of the massive wardrobe and find, like something out of *Alice through the Looking Glass*, the way into the bathroom.

The castle's rooms are bursting with antique furniture and massive four-poster beds, mostly dating from the castle's heyday in Jacobean times. Bedrooms have split levels, secret panels, massive carved inglenook fireplaces, and rich period drapes. Newly converted rooms around the courtyard have beams and a chintzy charm.

The Black Knight Restaurant, with its arches and tented ceiling, is a unique visual experience and full of atmosphere. But it can be very busy, so dining there may be a prolonged experience. There is a cosy bar, with library shelves, display cases full of objets d'art and log fires. The Baron's Hall offers Elizabethan banquets at weekends, and the castle is a bustling place, at times a little reminiscent of something out of Disneyland.

However, it is an hotel not to be missed. It is set in six acres of park, next to a golf course, and also has an indoor swimming pool and sauna and a billiard room.

The Romans loved this area, near the most beautiful and unspoilt beaches in Britain. The compact city of Durham, with its ancient cathedral and castle, Newcastle, and Gateshead with its superb Metrocentre shopping complex, are within easy reach.

THE GHOST is 'The Lily of Lumley' – wife of Sir Ralph Lumley, who built the castle in 1392.

The North-East has always been a particularly violent corner of England, and Lady Lumley, known as 'The Lily', fell foul of the

Catholic Church by becoming a follower of the 'heretic' preacher John Wycliffe. Such rebelliousness was unheard of in an area where the 'Prince Bishops' held both spiritual and temporal power, and The Lily was duly murdered by a visiting priest. He disposed of her body by shoving her down a convenient well.

That well is now covered by the shower cubicle in the bathroom of Room 45, and The Lily is said to have been seen rising from her watery grave by way of the shower cubicle and wafting into the corridor outside Rooms 45 and 46.

Both guests and staff claim to have witnessed this. But the stories of The Lily's wanderings go back many years and appearances by the ghost are recorded in the castle's chronicles.

Although Lumley Castle is a 'fun' place to stay, it can have the creepy sort of atmosphere that one might expect of a medieval building – and if I was taking a shower in Room 45 it might be a rather hurried one. I have stayed in Room 46, and found nothing odd about that; on the contrary it is extremely comfortable. But, whatever the reason, there is a noticeable 'cold spot' in the corridor outside Rooms 45 and 46.

Lumley Castle's wells seem to have led a rather unfortunate existence. The one in the lobby outside the bar – now floodlit in a gruesome shade of green – is claimed to have 'something nasty' which comes out occasionally, although nobody is saying what or when. And the second floor is said to be pervaded by the presence of the spirit of a murdered child. Of such stuff are legends made.

52 LYTHE HILL HOTEL   South East England

Petworth Road, Haslemere, Surrey GU27 3BQ
Telephone: 0428-651251
Telex: 858402

> *Rooms:* 26 double, 14 twin
> *Location:* Rural   *Price Range:* ££££
> *Restaurant:* Entente Cordiale (English and international) à la carte ££; table d'hôte £; Auberge de France (French) à la carte £££
> *Facilities:* Historic building; lifts; croquet; tennis; sauna; fishing

More than four centuries separate the two buildings that make up the Lythe Hill Hotel, in leafy Surrey. The main part of the hotel is a standard modern design around a courtyard, built in local beige stone. But the ancient half-timbered manor house, which is the hotel's prime restaurant, is a Tudor jewel just across the drive from the newer building.

In the newer part of the hotel is the main restaurant, which offers the best of English and traditional cuisine. The oak-panelled 'Auberge de France' restaurant in the Tudor farmhouse specialises in French cooking with the nouvelle cuisine touch, and has a terrace overlooking the hotel's gardens and lake.

Bedrooms in the new building are modern, comfortable and furnished in soft pastel shades. But the rooms in the Tudor building are all impressively furnished with period pieces, including one four-poster bed with the date 1614 carved on it. The Tudor Room is one of two suites with oak beams; the other is named after Anne of Cleves, the wife of King Henry VIII, who made the manor house her home when she was banished for supposed infidelity by the monarch, who later divorced her.

Visitors to Lythe Hill need hardly leave the 14 acres of grounds. Croquet, tennis, saunas, and fishing in the lake are all available.

Birds enjoy the grounds, too: pigeons still nest in the original loft now built into the new building, and a pair of swans grace the lake. Perhaps inevitably, the swans have been christened Basil and Sybil – but Lythe Hill bears no resemblance to Basil and Sybil Fawlty's 'Fawlty Towers'.

The Sussex downlands, with their pretty villages, are within easy reach of Lythe Hill, and there is horse-racing at Goodwood and polo at Cowdray Park. Arundel, with its antique shops, and Chichester with its cathedral, are an interesting excursion.

THE GHOST is said to be that of Anne of Cleves, King Henry VIII's fourth wife, who haunts the magnificent Tudor building which is used as the hotel's gourmet restaurant.

Above the restaurant, which is across a courtyard from the main hotel building, the owner has created two beautiful suites: the Anne of Cleves Suite and the Tudor Room. The former is supposedly haunted by Anne herself, who wafts from one old doorway to another. The fact that the doors were bricked up long ago doesn't bother this regal ghost – she goes straight through them anyway.

If you are feeling dubious, it should be stressed that the restaurant building was a Tudor manor house, to which Anne of Cleves was banished when she fell out of favour with Henry VIII. She was eventually divorced in 1540, and lived in retirement for a further 17 years until her death.

It should also be stressed that there is nothing spooky about either of the suites. I have slept in the Anne of Cleves suite and it is warm, homely and comfortable. If Anne did any wandering around in the night, she didn't wake me.

Guests are sometimes awakened, however, by the sound of a door banging down in the empty restaurant long after both diners and staff have departed. Mention it to the management next morning and you'll be told that it is a not unusual occurrence, and that all the doors were securely fastened. Mention it to the maitre d', and you might get a knowing smile. 'That wasn't a door banging, that was Anne,' I was told. 'She gets in some terrible tempers'. I expect it was a joke.

[53] THE MALT HOUSE

Heart of England

Broad Campden, Chipping Campden, Gloucestershire GL55 6UU
Telephone: 0386-840295

Rooms: 2 double, 2 twin
Location: Rural
Restaurant: en famille table d'hôte £
Facilities: Croquet; gardens

Price Range: ££

In one of the prettiest villages in England, three little houses dating from the 1600s have been lovingly restored and converted into one cosy and atmospheric guesthouse – the Malt House.

Mrs Pat Robinson has lavished much attention to detail in this cottage-style house, and provided every comfort for visitors. From the moment visitors enter the beamed hall, the cosiness and hospitality are apparent. Log fires warm the dining-room, where Pat Robinson serves gourmet meals based on French and English cuisine, but with her own country touch (nettle soup and venison, for example, often feature in season). These meals are served on a massive oak refectory table.

The drawing-room, too, is oak-beamed, and has an inglenook fireplace in which half a tree-trunk does not look out of place. Leather-covered furniture, a massive grandfather clock, and the views from the latticed windows all help to provide a peaceful atmosphere.

The four guest bedrooms are furnished in pretty chintzes and country-style period furniture.

The house is set in large gardens with a croquet lawn, a thatched summerhouse, and a kitchen garden that delights the eye as well as gracing the table. Beyond are cherry orchards, and flocks of rare poultry and some Jacob sheep.

The lovely, antique-shop-filled Cotswold villages are all around: Broadway, Bourton-on-the-Water and Moreton-in-Marsh are only a few miles away. Georgian Cheltenham, with its racecourse, is less than an hour's drive away, and Shakespeare's birthplace at Stratford-upon-Avon makes an interesting excursion.

THE GHOST is a poltergeist with a liking for bells. Poltergeists, which are often associated with children, can be a plague; this one seems harmless. It just loves bells. Even the slightest 'ping' of the telephone can set it off.

It has been there for centuries, almost since the houses were built. It loves Sundays: the sound of the bells pealing from the lovely Norman church opposite set it prancing about and knocking things over.

It is certainly a benevolent poltergeist. It likes dropping things but it doesn't like breaking them. So when the 'phone rings some household knick-knack – or even the 'phone itself – may be moved, but it won't be smashed.

Present owner Pat Robinson doesn't mind the spirit. But she does wish that it could be a little less active when she is busy with her guests. Many a time she has answered the summons of the little bell by the Visitors' Book in reception, only to find the bell on its side and no-one in the house but herself.

The spirit, rather like Peter Pan's Tinkerbell, is occasionally seen as a swift-moving and shimmering light. Tinkerbell started to die when no-one believed in her, but as Pat Robinson believes firmly in her poltergeist the light should go on shining for many years yet.

54 THE MANOR HOUSE HOTEL

Heart of England

Avenue Road, Royal Leamington Spa, Warwickshire CV31 3NJ
Telephone: 0926-423251
Fax: 0926-425933

> *Rooms:* include 28 double, 12 twin, 2 family rooms
> *Location:* Central   *Price Range:* ££
> *Restaurant:* Pavilion (international cuisine) à la carte ££;
>   table d'hôte £; Saddle Room (grills) £

A handsome red brick building, which started life as an hotel in 1847, the Manor House is as generously proportioned as one might expect from a place designed with crinoline wearers in mind.

The plasterwork ceilings, panelled walls and tall windows reflect the taste and comforts of grander times. Created when the spa town of Leamington was in its heyday – with guests coming from all over the country to take the waters in the Pump Room, as well as to see and be seen – the hotel is as busy a meeting place today as it was then.

The Pavilion Restaurant, with its ornate plaster ceiling, offers a wide range of international dishes, and the adjoining bars offer light snacks throughout the day as well as being cosy places in which to relax.

The hotel's 54 bedrooms have all been recently redecorated and refurbished, and offer all modern amenities, with delightful fresh and chintzy colour schemes echoing the period feel of the public rooms.

Set in the town centre, not far from the river, the hotel is only a short walk from the lovely Jephson Gardens and the Pump Rooms. Warwick, with its magnificent castle, and Shakespeare's birthplace in Stratford-upon-Avon, are only a short drive away. The big cities of Birmingham and Coventry, the latter boasting a beautiful cathedral, are also worth visiting. And Alton Towers, with its vast leisure park and white-knuckle rides, is a good day out for families.

THE GHOST is that of a Victorian housekeeper, wearing a long, grey uniform, who wanders the corridors on the second floor of both the old and new wings of the hotel.

The night porter has seen her, and so have several other members of the staff. Her appearance is always heralded by a chill.

The local story is that the housekeeper was prematurely retired whilst working at the Manor House when it was a private hotel in the town's heyday and died missing both her work and the company. Quite what she is doing in the new wing of the hotel, nobody can explain.

55 MARLEFIELD HOUSE

Lowlands

Eckford, by Kelso, Roxburghshire TD5 8ED, Scotland
Telephone: 05735-561
Fax: 05735-393

Rooms: 2 double, 2 twin, 3 family rooms
Location: Rural *Price Range:* ££
Restaurant: à la carte ££; table d'hôte £
Facilities: Historic building; extensive grounds

Once the Borders stronghold of a cattle-rustling family, Marlefield House still has at its heart the early twelfth-century fortified tower around which it has spread. The present-day house is a sturdy example of the Jacobite-French style of the 1700s, and has passed into the safe hands of John and Ann Taylor after having some highly colourful owners. The feuding Bennet family, for example, who died out after glorious exploits with the Duke of Marlborough in wars against the French; or the Marquis of Tweeddale, in the mid-nineteenth century; and the Hays family, of the Cunard Steamship Line.

Under the stewardship of the Taylors, Marlefield House has become a superb and intimate country house hotel, half-hidden

Marlefield House

behind a farm at the end of a long winding track not far from the lovely town of Kelso.

The hunt for the hotel is worthwhile. Locals beat a path to the door for the food – whether it is John Taylor's superb haute cuisine, based on local ingredients, or the simple but excellent-value bar meals.

The hotel has eight bedrooms, all spacious and beautifully furnished. Some retain the ornate plasterwork panelling of the Georgian era; one has a four-poster bed; all have luxurious touches like bathrobes and a wide range of toiletries. The magnificent staircase – designed, like the house windows, by Sir Christopher Wren – leads down to the cosy panelled bar, and the elegant dining room has all the grace of the eighteenth century from which the furniture comes.

The drawing room, on the first floor, commands lovely views over the park and Lowland hills, and contains the wonderful craftsmanship of Robert Adam, whose chisels carved the decorations and two doorways. The hall is panelled with the remains of the first Cunard steamship to be broken up.

Sports galore, ranging from shooting and fishing to horse-riding and golf, are all within easy reach. And historic towns like Jedburgh and Melrose, with its abbey, and the lovely scenery made popular by Sir Walter Scott, are on the doorstep.

THE GHOST is an unseen figure, which brushes past people in the hotel's stillroom – a sort of pantry – and, rather more publicly, in the passage outside the door leading into the ladies' loo.

Co-owner Ann Taylor and head waitress Ali have both experienced the phenomenon. John Taylor remains unconvinced, although presumably he does not have reason to visit the ladies' very often.

Both the spots where this unseen figure is sensed are very close to the entrance to an old tunnel, now blocked up, which dates from the seventeenth century. Like the ghost, the tunnel and its purpose are a bit of a mystery. It may have been something to do with smugglers, but the Taylors' theory is that it was a hidey-hole for Catholic priests during the troubled times of the Jacobite uprisings.

THE MERMAID HOTEL — South East England

Rye, Sussex
Telephone: 0797-223065
Telex: 957141

Rooms: include 17 double, 6 twin
Location: Central   *Price Range:* £££
Restaurant: à la carte £; table d'hôte £
Facilities: Historic building

Only in England could a 500-year-old hotel refer to itself as 'new'. The hotel is the Mermaid, in the ancient Cinque Port town of Rye, and the 'new' Mermaid was opened in 1420, replacing the original wattle-and-daub building that had offered hospitality to travellers since before 1300.

Today, the hotel retains many of its ancient features, including pre-1377 barrel-vaulted cellars which alone survived the fire started by French raiders that year which devastated the town. The inn's heyday was in Elizabethan times, and Queen Elizabeth I herself stayed there. But it was in the 1700s that the Mermaid became notorious, for it was the headquarters of a succession of gangs of smugglers who used this part of the coast to run their illicit cargoes ashore.

The Mermaid Hotel

There is no such turmoil in evidence at the Mermaid today. Its leaded windows and panelled rooms have a timeless peace about them, and the bar with its massive Giant's Fireplace is a cosy and atmospheric place to sit. The restaurant has lovely linenfold panelling, and offers a menu specialising in locally caught fish and Sussex lamb. And Dr Syn's Lounge is full of curiosities and antiques, mainly dating from the 1530s.

Both the public rooms and the bedrooms ar warmly furnished with a multitude of antiques. There are 28 bedrooms, mostly with en suite bathrooms, and in keeping with the building's half-timbered exterior they have historic beds, including three massive four-poster beds. The Elizabethan Chamber has the most handsome and ornate of these beds and the room, like many of the others, has secret panels in the walls. The Dr Syn Room, named for the smuggling vicar of the Thorndike novel, has panels behind a bookcase which lead to a secret passage down to the seashore. But the Mermaid has moved with the times, and besides such curiosities its guest rooms boast every modern comfort.

Rye and its neighbouring towns are full of fascinating history. Hastings was another smuggling centre and, like Canterbury with its magnificent cathedral, is only a short drive away. The lovely countryside of Kent and Sussex is all around for walking and sporting opportunities.

THE GHOST is a pair of spirits – and a combative pair, at that. One of the bedrooms in this ancient haunt of smugglers is often the scene of a spectral duel to the death, with the loser being dumped unceremoniously down a chute in the corner of the room.

Over the years, there have been many reports of this rather scary happening. Most recently, an American woman reported waking up to see two swarthy men in eighteenth-century dress in her room, fighting with swords. Paralysed with shock, she kept to her bed as the duel raged around the room. So vivid were the figures that it was several minutes before she realised that, for all their ferocity, the pair were making no sound.

Eventually, the stronger man prevailed. Killing his opponent with a vicious stroke of his cutlass, he rifled the presumed corpse's pockets before carrying him to a corner of the room, where he appeared to open a secret panel and deposit the corpse in the recess.

Next morning, when she told her tale, the guest discovered that several such murders had taken place in the inn in the 1740s, when the notorious Hawkshurst gang of smugglers defied everyone with their illegal activities, carousing and insolence. And her room did indeed have a secret panel, leading to an oubliette in the wall. In the past, bones have been found at the bottom of that oubliette.

Despite her experience, the brave American guest was quite willing to spend the rest of her holiday in the same room. But if you ask, the hotel staff tend to be rather reticent about which room it is that becomes a battleground on occasions. Suffice it to say that it overlooks the cobbled hill on which the Mermaid stands.

57 NEW HALL   Heart of England

Walmley Road, Sutton Coldfield, Warwickshire B75 7UU
Telephone: 021-378-2442
Fax: 021-378-4637

Rooms: include 25 double, 15 twin, 6 suites
Location: Suburban but tranquil   *Price Range:* £££££
Restaurant: à la carte £££; table d'hôte ££
Facilities: Historic building; lift; extensive grounds

New Hall

Surrounded by a lily-filled moat, the 800-year old manor house of mellow stone that is now New Hall Hotel looks like a picture from the top of a chocolate box. The house, complete with turrets and domes, bridges and battlements, grew up near seven springs of water on land granted to the then Earl of Warwick by King Henry I in 1126. Later, King Henry VIII almost met his death while hunting in the park when a wild boar charged him; he was saved by an arrow shot by a daughter of the house, and in gratitude granted her the return of confiscated lands and the use of a Tudor rose in the family's escutcheon.

Of such stuff is romance made, and the present-day hotel run by Ian and Caroline Parkes is full of tapestries, stained glass, antiques and memorabilia of the families who have lived here over the centuries. Set in 26 acres of gardens, the hotel has public rooms ranging from the intimate to the vast. The Great Hall has an ornate ceiling decorated with heraldic crests. The vaulted cellars recently yielded a treasure in the shape of a hoard of nineteenth-century prints unique to New Hall, and many of these can be seen in the hotel. Other treasures and works of art once belonging to the Hall have been brought back to complete the authentic picture.

The hotel has 46 bedrooms, all furnished with original pieces and including some very stately four-poster beds. Baskets of fruit and wine in each bedroom are among the luxury touches. Unlike many hoteliers, Ian and Caroline Parkes make a stay at New Hall feel like staying in a private – and very grand – home. The restaurant in the old Dining Room, which overlooks the moat, has open fires and a delicious range of dishes. And if you chance to look out of the window while dining, you might just see the chef rowing across the moat to gather the watercress that grows there for your salad.

Despite its grandeur, and its country feel, New Hall is close to the centre of Sutton Coldfield. The great cities of Birmingham and Coventry are nearby, and Stratford-upon-Avon and Warwick are popular places to visit.

THE GHOST, surprisingly, is to be found in the grounds of this hotel, rather than in the ancient and atmospheric building itself. And, also surprisingly, this ghost is not a headless body but what can only be called a bodyless head. Over the years, a number of frightened people have reported seeing this head rolling about in the grounds beyond the moat.

The story goes that, in 1745, a servant of the Chadwick family living at New Hall was suspected of being a Catholic and a Jacobite sympathiser by the English armies, who came across him as they were returning south under the leadership of 'Butcher' Cumberland after their defeat of Bonnie Prince Charlie. The poor unfortunate, who had a speech defect and couldn't defend himself, was summarily beheaded. His body was taken away for burial, but the severed head was tossed casually into an oak tree.

Reports of the ghostly head, rolling around the grounds in a vain search for the body from which it has been separated, began soon afterwards. Cynics scoffed.

But in 1827 something very strange happened. Estate workers removing old and damaged trees outside New Hall felled an ancient oak. And as it toppled majestically to the ground there rolled from a hidden hollow... a human skull! Closer examination showed that the owner of the skull had suffered from a cleft palate.

The spectral head is still seen, at dusk, wafting mistily across the park in search of its final resting place alongside the missing body.

58 OCKENDEN MANOR — South East England

Ockenden Lane, Cuckfield, Sussex RH17 5LD
Telephone: 0444-416111
Fax: 0444-415549

> *Rooms:* include 11 double, 2 twin
> *Location:* Central   *Price Range:* ££££
> *Restaurant:* à la carte ££; table d'hôte £
> *Facilities:* Historic building; extensive grounds

This medieval manor house is now the lovely and welcoming Ockenden Manor Hotel. It has a mixed history, and its first recorded owners were the Okyndens, whose title to the house passed to the Burrell family in the seventeenth century. A later son of the Burrells, Timothy, kept a journal which gives a fascinating insight

Ockenden Manor

into the daily life in the house during his time, and it records the many alterations made to keep the house 'up to date'.

Those alterations include the installation of some fine panelling and stained glass, much of which is still in place today in the hotel's lovely restaurant with its painted ceiling. There, the dishes owe a great deal to the timeless ingredients of English cooking – fresh game and local lamb, for instance, cooked with herbs from the Manor gardens.

The lounge is beautifully furnished with antique furniture and heavy drapes which add to the historic atmosphere, and the personal touch of the present owners, the Goodmans, is everywhere in the objets d'art and mementoes which decorate the rooms. The staff are very attentive, and contribute a great deal to the warmth of the house and its welcome.

Ockenden Manor has 14 bedrooms, all with typical English Christian names instead of a number. Elizabeth and Charles, for instance, have antique four-poster beds; Elizabeth and Thomas are reached by private staircases; the Master suite has its own sitting room; and all the bedrooms enjoy sweeping views over the Sussex countryside. Needless to say, all bedrooms have every modern amenity.

The Manor has more than five acres of grounds for guests to enjoy, and these are gradually being restored to their original Elizabethan style. Cuckfield itself is a pretty Tudor village, and the beautiful gardens at Leonardslee, Nymans, and Sissinghurst are an attraction for those interested in horticulture. The historic towns of Tunbridge Wells and Chichester are interesting excursions, and the delights of Brighton and the Sussex coastal resorts are only a short drive away.

THE GHOST is that of a Grey Lady – who is often sensed, as well as seen, as a kindly presence in the 'Elizabeth' guest bedroom.

She is thought to be the shade of a young girl who, having been forbidden to meet her lover, took to subterranean subterfuge to keep their rendezvous. Ockenden Manor has secret passages running from its cellars to the cellars of the nearby Kings Head inn, in South Street. Built in the early years of the house's history, at a time when there were religious struggles in England, the tunnels were already ancient and in disrepair when the girl passed along them in the nineteenth century.

One day, though, the house shook with underground rumblings, and it was noticed that the girl was missing. Her body was eventually discovered in one of the tunnels which had collapsed and crushed her to death.

There have also been strange presences felt coming from the Priest's Hole, built cunningly into the great chimney on the south wall, near a cubby-hole sized room which was used as a chapel.

But it is undoubtedly the Grey Lady who is seen about the bedroom corridor. She was seen recently by a night porter on his rounds, who was amazed to find her opening and closing the bedroom doors. Quite what made her behave so inhospitably on this one occasion is not known.

59 THE OLD DEANERY South East England

Battle, East Sussex TN33 0AQ
Telephone: 04246-4409

Rooms: 3 double, 1 twin
Location: Central but tranquil   *Price Range:* ££
Restaurant: none
Facilities: Historic building; gardens

The Old Deanery

There have been deans in Battle almost since *the* battle in 1066, and an early Abbot of the beautiful Battle Abbey founded the nearby parish church of St Mary's, complete with its neighbouring house for the dean, in 1115.

Nowadays, The Old Deanery is no longer the dean's residence, but an attractive and highly atmospheric private house offering bed and breakfast in its four guest bedrooms. The present house is Elizabethan, on older foundations, and full of ancient stonework, twisted beams, and quaint and characterful corners. Full of character, too, is the owner, Kay Coomber, who is passionately interested in the history of her home. Her breakfasts reflect that history, for they include local ingredients and historic dishes like frumenty (a sort of fruit-flavoured porridge) and spicy home-made sausages.

The massive oak front door swings shut behind visitors, who find themselves in a comfortable parlour, with chaises-longue, shelves of books, a piano, a drinks cupboard featuring mulled mead, and a music library. The breakfast room is country kitchen-style, the dresser crammed with old china.

Upstairs, the Watson Suite has a stunning designer bathroom with double whirlpool bath, and the Naylor Suite has a lovely pink-toned decor surrounding its four-poster bed and whirlpool bathroom. Views from the rooms are over the Deanery gardens to the church and Abbey.

The Old Deanery's gardens were on the site of the Battle of Hastings. They contain two wells, one edged with carved stones from earlier deaneries on the site. Domestic pets include two large but friendly dogs and a pond full of koi carp.

Battle has its famous Abbey, battlefield sites, and many restaurants and pubs serving evening meals, as well as pretty speciality shops. Nearby Hastings, and the other seaside resorts of East Sussex, are within easy reach, and there is lots of wonderful walking on the South Downs.

THE GHOST is of a beautiful young woman who enters through the front door and crosses the hall towards the stairs. She was seen by a number of ecclesiastical residents and their servants when the house really was a deanery, before 1986. She has also been heard playing the piano, which the present owner has placed in the residents' lounge conveniently close to the front door.

She is probably Elizabeth Boyes, who died in the 1870s, aged 26. Elizabeth, from Hawkshurst, moved to the Hastings area for her health and fell in love with Lieutenant Charles Lamb, the commander of a revenue cutter, whose family lived at the Old Deanery.

But Elizabeth's father disapproved of the match and the couple had to meet illicitly at the Lovers' Seat, a picturesque spot on the cliffs at Fairlight, which was destroyed in a cliff fall in 1961. They eventually eloped to London and were married in January 1786. But the romance had a sad ending because Elizabeth died soon after her marriage, and her husband was drowned at sea in 1814.

That is the story that the deans have passed down – although, to be fair, other local reports suggest that Elizabeth lived to a ripe old age. If that is the case, another possible contender for the role of beautiful spectre is Martha Nairn, who married into the music-loving Webster family which had been cursed by the monks of Battle Abbey because of some hanky-panky with their treasures and lands during the Dissolution of the Monasteries.

The Websters, who all died by fire or water as the monks had predicted, were buried in a crypt in St Mary's parish church, right next to the Old Deanery. Some grave-robbing in the crypt may have led to Martha's wanderings, if such they are.

One of the deans who lived in the Old Deanery, Dr John Wythines, is also supposed to haunt the house. Dr Wythines was something of a local black sheep in the early seventeen century – accused of not administering or taking communion for two years and of 'favouring the old religion' (ie: paganism). He died in May 1615 and his likeness appears on one of the brasses in St Mary's Church, so if you see him it should be easy to check his identity.

Such an old house is bound to have a stock of spooky stories. It is a fact that the owners' two dogs – a bull mastiff and an alsatian – won't go into the garage at one end of the house, from which a secret tunnel is believed to lead to the church and on to Battle Abbey. And a French journalist staying in the Watson Suite recently complained that his sleep was disturbed by the cries and clatter of an invisible battle. Odd, because documents at the house suggest that it, rather than Battle Abbey, stands on the spot that was the Norman lines during the Battle of Hastings in 1066.

60 THE OLD SWAN HOTEL

Yorkshire & Humberside

Swan Road, Harrogate, North Yorkshire HG1 2SR
Telephone: 0423 500055
Fax: 0423-501154

Rooms: include 44 double, 51 twin
Location: Central *Price Range:* ££££
Restaurant: Library Restaurant (international cuisine) à la carte ££;
    table d'hôte £; Wedgewood Room (table d'hôte only) £
Facilities: Lift; business centre; tennis; croquet; putting; gardens

The Old Swan, a huge old coaching house which was a favourite stopping-place for royalty on their travels in Georgian times, sits proudly in the centre of the lovely spa town of Harrogate. 'Taking the waters' of the spa was a luxurious as well as a health-giving experience for noble guests in the eighteenth and nineteenth centuries. And crime-writer Agatha Christie made the hotel her hideaway in 1926, when she mysteriously 'disappeared' for a considerable time.

The hotel has a wealth of elegant ceilings and panelled rooms, richly furnished in period style, with lovely brass chandeliers, old prints and gilt mirrors. The Lounge Bar, with its plasterwork panels, offers a retreat where cream teas, as well as drinks, can be enjoyed, and is a pleasant place to sit. The Lounge itself, with comfortable velvet-covered chairs, is a relaxing spot.

The hotel has two restaurants, plus a range of function rooms. The Library restaurant – complete with book-lined alcoves, stained glass windows and antique mahogany furniture – offers a classic menu with an international flavour. The large Wedgwood Room, whose plaster mouldings are all in the unmistakeable style of the pottery genius whose name it shares, offers a fresh table d'hote menu daily.

The hotel's 114 bedrooms are all newly refurbished in a style which echoes the building's Georgian past: period furniture in warm mahogany complements beds with drapes falling from the ceiling in tones harmonising with the spreads and with each room's particular ambience. And there is a very grand two-bedroomed suite.

Harrogate is a town with much to offer; an entertainment programme that London might envy, antique shops, and 'Betty's famous tea-shop which is almost a place of pilgrimage. The Yorkshire Dales and the North York Moors are within easy reach, and York itself is an interesting excursion.

THE GHOST is more a happening than a figure. Someone, or something, has a habit of upsetting the chambermaids' carts while they are cleaning the hotel's third-floor rooms. But there is never anyone in sight.

This phenomenon has been going on for years, with a succession of maids getting irate, or distraught, or just plain giggly, as they hear the well-known crash of their supply-trolley toppling over in the corridor while they are making up the guest rooms.

Many traps and watches have been set, but no human agency has ever been detected and no obvious natural phenomena, like high winds, can explain these occurrences. One theory, held by a recent public relations manager at the hotel, was that in the 1920s a maid was dismissed for supposedly taking items of negligible value from guests' rooms, and her spirit has ever since been getting her own back on colleagues who 'told' on her. She adds to their work by making them scurry around collecting up towels, toilet rolls and tablets of soap which she has scattered around the third-floor corridors.

But that is just a theory. What is certain is that both chambermaids and guests often experience the phenomenon. But no damage is done, and everyone seems to take the spirit's meddling in good part.

61 PANNANICH WELLS HOTEL

Tayside & Grampian

South Deeside Road, Ballater, Royal Deeside AB3 5SJ, Scotland
Telephone: 03397-55018
Fax: 03397-55038

> *Rooms:* include 3 double, 1 twin
> *Location:* Rural
> *Restaurant:* table d'hôte £
> *Facilities:* Grounds
> *Price Range:* £££

The South Deeside road once ran right through the cluster of buildings that is now the Pannanich Wells Hotel, but the road has been moved and the buildings linked up around a central courtyard to form the modern hotel. Dating from 1760, the original inn grew up with a reputation based on the quality of its waters – Deeside's big attraction before it became a royal holiday haven. Mineral springs still rise from the hillside behind the hotel's main bedroom wing.

The low, granite buildings are full of atmosphere – as owners Chris and Val Norton say: 'Anyone *accepted* by the place will love it!' The romantic 'mad, bad and dangerous to know' poet Lord Byron lingered here, and mooned out of the windows in what is now the bar after a local lass. Harry Lauder also visited, and even Queen Victoria drank Pannanich waters and praised their health-giving qualities.

Today, the hotel has pleasant, comfortable and simply furnished rooms. The bar and dining-room are on one side of the old highway-cum-courtyard giving views over the valley of the Dee, and a hallway links these rooms with the neat bedrooms on the other side of the road. Each of the five bedrooms has a harmonising and restful colour scheme, and Val Norton makes sure that each has fresh flowers and a bowl of fruit to welcome guests.

The young staff are eager to please, and the restaurant serves excellent steaks and an international menu. Portions are hefty enough to satisfy a healthy Highland appetite – a Pannanich tradition dating back to the days when Queen Victoria's controversial ghillie, John Brown, worked as a stable-boy for the inn.

The hotel is just across the river from Ballater and only a few miles from the royal holiday home of Balmoral Castle, so it is well-placed for guests to enjoy the scenic and sporting delights of the Dee valley.

Wildlife enthusiasts will find much to excite them in the neighbouring glens like Glen Muick (pronounced 'Mick'); there is fine walking, stalking and fishing; and Aberdeen and Braemar are both less than an hour's drive away. The Braemar Gathering, on the first Saturday in September, is the area's leading social event and the Queen always attends.

THE GHOST is of a woman, dressed in grey, and has been seen by both the present owners of the hotel and their predecessors.

The 'Grey Lady' emerges from Room 1, leans on the bannisters at the top of the stairs, goes down the stairs, and goes out into what was the main road. She is also seen walking down the road towards Ballater, but only goes as far as an oak tree which leans across the road a few hundred yards from the hotel.

Nobody seems to know who the Grey Lady is, although the hotel's reputation for being haunted is well known in Ballater. Often, the spectre is heard rather than seen: doors open and close mysteriously, the sound of furniture being moved comes from empty rooms, footsteps are heard, and a child staying in Room 1 complained of a 'breathing' noise. Nobody has ever seen anything in the bedroom, but it is often inexplicably scented with an old-fashioned perfume.

It would appear that the Grey Lady is not the Pannanich Wells Hotel's only intangible guest. An old lady has been seen sitting and spinning on a hillside behind the hotel, close to the springs which give it is name. Approach her and she vanishes.

But that is nothing compared with the quite recent experience of a former owner of the hotel, who late one night went to check the pinball machine and snooker table in a room near the bar which was used for such amusements. The room is now designated Bedroom 6, but at the time of writing is unused and awaiting refurbishment.

As he entered the room, the former owner was astonished to see three disreputable-looking characters sitting at a round table playing cards. A knife was stuck into the centre of the table, and a peat fire smouldered malodorously behind them. The landlord told the men that it was past closing time and asked them to leave, but they glared at him and continued with their game. So he stepped outside, called for a waiter to come and help him, then stepped back into the room.

Apart from the pinball machine and snooker table, it was empty. No card players; no circular table; no knife; and the fireplace, he now recalled, had been bricked up years ago. He also recalled the old local stories about that room, which told how a man had been knifed to death there during a game of cards....

62 THE PARK INTERNATIONAL HOTEL

East Midlands

Humberstone Road, Leicester, Leicestershire LE5 3AT
Telephone: 0533 620471
Fax: 0533-514211

> *Rooms:* include 47 double, 40 twin, 11 family rooms
> *Location:* Central   *Price Range:* £££
> *Restaurant:* Tapestry Grill (international cuisine) à la carte ££; table d'hôte £; Strikes (coffee shop) £
> *Facilities:* Lift

The Midlands city of Leicester was once a centre of the shoe trade; today one of the huge factories, which once belonged to a major chain of manufacturers and retailers, is home to the Park International Hotel.

The old part of the building, bombed during the Second World Was, has been restored in its original style, and a spectacular tower houses the entrance lobby and a new bedroom wing, making this a large and business-oriented hotel. Its 200 bedrooms have all modern amenities, and are furnished in pleasant pastel colour schemes, with matching drapes and quilted bedspread giving a feeling of warmth and comfort.

The hotel's two restaurants match its ambience. The modern, coffee-shop-style Strikes offers a bright spot for a quick meal, while the Tapestry Grill features a more traditional and relaxed style of dining. The latter has a wide-ranging menu of international favourites and is good value. There are two bars, too, with the Melton Bar matching the traditional atmosphere and the International Bar being the hotel's lively meeting place.

Leicester has many attractive and historic places to visit – a medieval Guildhall with many Tudor features, and the roman remains of a forum and baths which include the largest remaining Roman building in the country at Jewry Wall. The costume museum in a fifteenth-century merchant's house is also worth seeing. The city is a good touring base: the castles of Kenilworth and Warwick are within easy reach, as is the site of the battle of Bosworth where there is now an interpretive trail. The cathedral city of Lincoln, and Southwell with its Norman minster, are also interesting visits.

THE GHOST is that of a nightwatchman, who had a flat inside the building when it was a Freeman Hardy and Willis shoe factory. During the Second World War the factory was bombed, and the top corner of the building where the flat was situated received a direct hit. The nightwatchman was killed.

Since then, there have been persistent reports of a misty figure wafting though that area and diners in the restaurant – which is right below the ill-fated flat – have heard the sound of crying coming from above their heads.

Sad though this spirit may be, he also seems to be suffering the pangs of hunger. In 1990 the head chef stepped into a walk-in refrigerator to fetch some ingredients for the evening meal, and was alarmed to discover that he was being followed by the misty figure of a man in working clothes. Unnerved, the chef promptly fled.

⟦63⟧ PARKHILL HOTEL South of England
Beaulieu Road, Lyndhurst, Hampshire SO43 7FZ
Telephone: 070328-2944
Fax: 070328-3268

Rooms: include 19 doubles/twins
Location: Rural *Price Range:* £££
Restaurant: à la carte ££; table d'hôte ££
Facilities: Croquet; swimming pool; extensive grounds

The site of Parkhill Hotel was once a Roman fort. Nowadays the grounds surrounding the hotel, in the New Forest, are all manicured lawns and neat flowerbeds. And the house is a far cry from the medieval hunting lodge that the fort became. It is now an imposing Georgian gentleman's residence, built as the country home of the Duke of Clarence in 1740. In the nineteenth century it was the home of the then Master of the New Forest Hounds, who restored and extended the house. And now it is an excellent hotel.

Parkhill Hotel has an easy informality about it, with attentive and very professional young staff for whom nothing seems to be too much trouble. The public rooms are elegantly decorated with soft furnishings that complement the plasterwork of the ceilings and walls. There are several lounges and reading rooms, well stocked with easy chairs and the day's newspapers.

The restaurant is an airy room opening out on to the sweeping lawns, and if you step outside the hotel's family of ducks is likely to come visiting. The menu is international, but specialises in the fresh ingredients of the New Forest, especially venison and other game.

There are 20 bedrooms, including three suites in the old Coach House block. All are furnished with antiques and are extremely comfortable, and the private bathrooms have a touch of novelty in their design – one has a distinctly mermaid-like quality.

There are ten acres of gardens and woodlands to stroll in, a croquet lawn, and a heated open-air pool. For the more energetic there are horse-riding and golf nearby.

Parkhill is actually inside the New Forest itself, and the park's shaggy wild ponies can be found practically on the doorstep. The area is a rambler's delight, and Portsmouth, with its maritime heritage, Southampton and Bournemouth are all only a short drive away. Beaulieu, and the sailing centre of Bucklers Hard, are also nearby.

THE GHOST is that of Christine, who worked as a chambermaid at Parkhill in late Victorian times, when it was still a private house.

Christine died in a bath in the house, although it is no longer clear whether she was murdered or committed suicide. In either event she must have had a strong attachment to the house, because she still stalks the corridors. But, now that Parkhill is such a warm and hospitable hotel, it is impossible to imagine that she is anything other than a benign presence.

One male guest was not so sure. The reception staff report that he fled from Room 1 after waking up and finding Christine leaning over his bed. But that incident, as far as is known, was an isolated one.

64 PONDEN HALL Yorkshire & Humberside
Stanbury, nr Haworth, West Yorkshire
Telephone: 0535-644154

> *Rooms:* 2 double, 1 family room
> *Location:* Rural   *Price Range:* £
> *Restaurant:* en famille table d'hote £
> *Facilities:* Extensive grounds

A wild and windswept panorama greets visitors to Ponden Hall. Set high on the Yorkshire moors above the little town of Haworth, the long, low, granite hall is now a simple and homely small hotel, much loved by walkers and lovers of wide open spaces.

Ponden Hall has another attraction: it not only lies just a few miles from the home of the literary Bronte family but was actually the model for Thrushcross Grange in Emily Brontë's dramatic novel *Wuthering Heights*. Emily herself was a frequent visitor to

Ponden Hall, and the house still has an atmosphere recognisable to devotees of the Brontë family's novels.

But for all that, present owners Brenda and Roderick Taylor have made the house a warm and hospitable place, with many touches that make guests feel part of the family. The stone-flagged hall has a huge log fire to brighten its decor, and Brenda Taylor serves hearty home cooking in her family-style dining-room.

The house has only three guest bedrooms, and these are very simply but comfortably furnished. There are two shared bathrooms for guests.

With gardens and paddocks at the end of the tree-lined drive, and a reservoir as its neighbour, Ponden Hall has a rural atmosphere. The lovely countryside is all around, and the cities of York, with its Minster, and Bradford with its museums and industrial heritage, are interesting places to visit.

THE GHOST is that of an old man, who walks the upper corridors of the Hall and who is said to appear when a member of the Heaton family which once owned the house is about to die.

Ponden Hall dates back some 400 years, and for much of that time was in the ownership of the Heatons. Even in Victorian times it was well-known and recorded in the neighbourhood that when 'Old Grey Beard' – as he has been called over the years – appeared in the passageways of Ponden Hall, it spelt impending tragedy and death for one of the members of the family.

The present owners, Roderick and Brenda Taylor, were not put off by this tale when they bought the house some 15 years ago. And very soon they and some friends became aware they were not alone in the house – a presence was often felt, although there was nothing tangible to account for it.

It must have been Old Grey Beard giving the new owners the once-over, for one dark night Roderick Taylor was alone in the upstairs corridor when an elderly man, dressed in dark clothing, brushed past him. Assuming it to be one of the builders working in the house at the time, Roderick turned to speak to the figure – and watched it disappear through a wall.

This figure has not been seen since, and it seems that Old Grey

Beard was only making the acquaintance of the Taylors – for no dire events followed his appearance and none has happened since. But his presence is still sometimes noticed, as if someone were just keeping an eye on things.

65 PRESTBURY HOUSE HOTEL

Heart of England

The Burgage, Prestbury, Cheltenham, Gloucestershire GL52 3DN
Telephone: 0242-529533
Fax: 0242-227076

> *Rooms:* include 5 double, 12 twin
> *Location:* Suburban but peaceful   *Price Range:* ££
> *Restaurant:* à la carte ££; table d'hôte £
> *Facilities:* Business centre; gardens

Not a horseshoe's throw from Cheltenham Racecourse lies the pleasingly Georgian solidity of Prestbury House. Its roots date back to Elizabethan times, but the present house was built in 1700 after the ravages of the Civil War. A comfortable manor house in style, Prestbury House has many original features and the present owners, Jackie Gorrie and husband Stephen Witbourn, have filled the rooms with antiques. They are busily refurbishing the hotel, which Jackie's father bought from the Capel family who had owned it for hundreds of years.

The hotel has a comfortable lounge, and a panelled bar from which a thick, low, oak door – part of the early Elizabethan house – leads to the delightfully intimate Oak Room, used for dining or functions. The main restaurant is next door, in the cool plaster-worked Georgian dining-room. The food is excellent: the chef's platter of fresh vegetables is a meal in itself besides looking attractive.

Prestbury House has 18 bedrooms, all of them spacious and comfortable. There is a four-poster-bedded room, and some rooms have whirlpool baths. All have nice touches like a full tea service. The newer rooms are in the Coach House, across the courtyard.

Prestbury House Hotel

Scattered around the main house are some of the Gorrie family's treasures – including a carved sideboard in an upstairs lounge which takes pride of place.

Many people visit Cheltenham in general, and Prestbury House in particular, for the racing. But there is no need to go far from this comfortable base for exercise: the hotel offers horse-riding from a nearby stables; there is good golf on local courses. Prestbury House also has two acres of secluded gardens.

Horse-racing apart, Cheltenham is a lovely city, with its Montpelier area renowned for its speciality shops and high fashion boutiques. The Cotswolds are within easy reach, and Bath and Bristol are a comfortable drive away.

THE GHOST is that of a Royalist despatch rider, caught and killed by Cromwell's troops outside the front door of the hotel during the Civil War. His horse is still heard galloping through the courtyard in front of the old stable block in the early hours of the morning.

Owner Jackie Gorrie says many guests have heard the hoofbeats, but she is a pragmatic person and says: 'We are only just around the corner from Cheltenham Racecourse, and lots of horses get exercised early in the morning around here.' Even more prosaically, her husband has turned the stables into a conference centre.

But the couple are rather less jocular about another story connected with the hotel. During the 1970s, plumbers working in a room not regularly used by the hotel rushed out claiming that an old man with a white beard had waved a stick at them and shouted: 'Get out of here! Get out!' When they were persuaded to return, the room was empty. The plumbers were not the first to see this fierce phantom – but who he is and what he is doing in the hotel is not known.

Perhaps one should not be too surprised by his presence, because Prestbury – according to local ghost-hunter Bob Meredith – is the most haunted village in England. He claims to have identified a dozen spirits, compared with the eight or nine claimed by Pluckley, in Kent, which is officially Britain's spookiest spot.

Bob Meredith, it is important to add, is not one of the lunatic fringe of ghost-hunters: he is a teacher with an interest in folklore who has dug up many old and hair-raising local tales. Happily, he tells a good story himself, and his best involves another of Prestbury's horsey hauntings.

This time, it seems, the horse – complete with rider – was seen as well as heard, at what is now a road junction near Prestbury House. In the nineteenth century the alarmed villagers called in a priest to exorcise this nocturnal spirit but, according to Bob Meredith, the priest thought the whole thing was rubbish, rushed through the exorcism service, and missed out some vital point.

Now the road junction is still haunted. By half a horse!

66 REDWORTH HALL   Northumbria

Redworth, nr Newton Aycliffe, County Durham DL5 6NL
Telephone: 0388-772442
Fax: 0388-775112

> *Rooms:* include 61 double, 36 twin
> *Location:* Rural   *Price Range:* £££
> *Restaurant:* à la carte ££; table d'hôte £; Medieval Banquets £
> *Facilities:* Historic building; lift; leisure centre; extensive grounds

A handsome Jacobean mansion in the 'Land of the Prince Bishops', Redworth Hall is now a handsome country house hotel with its own leisure club for guests. The main house has 17 historic bedrooms, but attractive new wings increase the total number of rooms to 100 and an impressive choice of rooms.

The atmosphere has not been spoilt by the new extensions, for the 25 acres of ground provide plenty of room for expansion. The original hall was built in the late seventeenth century for the Crosier family, whose only daughter married into the Surtees family, a warrior clan who had fought at the battle of Agincourt and whose crest – complete with the Prince of Wales' feathers awarded for their part in the battle – appears in the carvings and stained glass everywhere in the Hall. After the Second World War the house passed from the Surtees into the keeping of the local authority, who ran it as an approved school for some years. Then came its careful and costly restoration, so that Redworth Hall now reflects much of its former glory.

There are comfortable lounges, and a restaurant cleverly constructed under a glass roof in an interior courtyard. The massive Servants' Hall and Baronial Hall (complete with minstrels' gallery and echoing flagstones) are the scene of medieval feasts, with a County Durham flavour. The restaurant itself offers a buffet-style breakfast, and its dinners feature specialities of the north-east of England, such as a tasty leek pudding.

The new bedrooms are very comfortable indeed, and those in the older part of the hotel have period four-poster beds, antique grandfather clocks, and other treasures.

The hotel's new leisure club offers a large swimming pool and every sort of health activity, and has a fun room for children. There is good walking in the grounds, where visitors might still find a Civil War cannonball or two, and the historic city of Durham, with its castle and cathedral, and the fascinating Bowes Museum, are only a short drive away.

THE GHOST is not one ghost, but a whole creepy crowd of them. So many stories are told about Redworth hall that on a recent Hallowe'en, the manager called in teams of ghost-busters and mediums, and offered a £5,000 reward to anyone who could prove that the hotel was haunted. The mediums saw spirits and the ghost-busters saw ghosts – but I and a number of other independent observers saw nothing and, at the time of writing, the cash is still in the kitty.

Redworth Hall has been in turn a private house, an approved school, and an hotel – and there are stories and spooks to match. Chief ghost seems to be 'Lady Catherine', who jumped to her death from the top of the tower in the mid-nineteenth century and who is thought to be the 'Lady in Grey' who has been seen by many former residents and by staff both past and present.

The Lady in Grey is a benign presence, who seems to be trying to guide people towards the happy life that she obviously lacked. Mrs Annie Watson, who was a servant at Redworth Hall when it was a private house, recalls sleeping in what is now Room 26 – a staff room – in the 1920s and seeing the Lady in Grey walk across the room and stand beside the cot in which Mrs Watson's child was sleeping. She describes the apparition as being 'well-dressed and kindly-looking'.

A similar sighting was reported a few years later by a seamstress working in the same room. So it is hardly surprising that Room 26 is not particularly popular with staff. The trouble is: in an hotel like Redworth Hall, where else do you go? In Rooms 5 and 9, china is rattled by unseen hands; the connecting door between Rooms 11 and 12 opens and closes of its own accord and the TV set has a life of its own; a baby is heard crying and coughing in empty rooms; a hazy figure is sometimes seen standing beside the fireplace in a small drawing-room; and another hazy figure is seen in front of the fire in the restaurant. And if thoughts of that little lot don't keep you awake, then perhaps the phantom piper will.

Not everybody takes these stories seriously. Mrs Watson's brother, William, was left to 'babysit' the empty house whilst working there as a gamekeeper, and claims that as he pulled off his boots and got ready for bed (in Room 26, of course), the door creaked open and a sepulchral voice said: 'William, there's only me and thee here'. 'Aye', retorted William, as he scrabbled to get dressed, 'and as soon as I get these boots back on there'll be only thee!'

67 THE REGENCY HOTEL South East England

28 Regency Square, Brighton, Sussex, BN1 2FH
Telephone: 0273-202690
Fax: 0273-220438

> *Rooms:* include 7 double, 2 twin
> *Location:* Central *Price Range:* ££
> *Restaurant:* table d'hôte by arrangement £

A Regency terrace of white stuccoed houses contains the Regency Hotel, not far from the Royal Pavilion in the heart of the seaside resort of Brighton. As fashionable now as then, Brighton gained fame as a bathing place when the Prince Regent, later George IV, was advised to take a sea cure – and society slavishly followed him

The Regency Hotel

to the seaside.

In the wake of royalty came the holidaymakers, and the streets of the town blossomed with guest houses and hotels. The Regency is a small private hotel, which offers simple but very comfortable accommodation. The lounge bar makes a pleasant place for an evening drink, and the breakfast room doubles as dining-room for those guests who have requested one of the hotel's excellent evening meals. There is a distinct period flavour to the decor and the furnishings and there are old prints on the walls.

The 13 bedrooms are well-equipped and comfortably furnished. The Regency Suite, overlooking the square, is very spacious, and has a romantic half-tester bed with elegant drapes, and its bay window catches the sun. All the bedrooms have every modern amenity.

Brighton has an entertainment programme to rival that of any major city, and its shopping, in the old 'Lanes' as well as in the modern shopping streets, is excellent. The delights of the Sussex countryside are all around, and there is good walking on the South Downs and a wide range of sporting possibilities in the area. The many beaches of the south coast are within easy reach.

THE GHOST is that of a poor crippled girl, who lived in the front room on the first floor of the hotel when it was a private lodging house. She died in a leap from her window on to the paving stones below, in the closing years of the Victorian era.

At that time, gas was a new-fangled thing in houses, and Regency Square had only recently been connected to the supply. The poor girl, getting a whiff of the pungent gas, and having been thoroughly alarmed by tales of leaks and subsequent explosions, quite lost her head in fear and panicked. Seeing the window as her only means of escape from the disaster she imagined overtaking her at any moment, she jumped out – and was killed instantly.

She has often been seen by staff and guest in the room she once occupied, now the Regency Suite. And a pair of her clogs can still be seen in the hotel bar.

But she is seen less and less frequently nowadays. It is thought she must have been lonely and looking for company. Recently, guests reported seeing another phantom, this time of a little old lady, who has been identified as the landlady of the lodging house at the time of the girl's death. The old lady and the girl have been seen together moving around the first floor rooms, seemingly quite happy in each other's company.

Whether visitors to the hotel today can see them or not, they are still around. No dog or cat will willingly venture on to the first floor, and have often bristled and appeared to watch unseen passers-by in that area of the hotel.

68 THE ROYAL HOTEL   South of England

Belgrave Road, Ventnor, Isle of Wight PO38 1JJ
Telephone: 0983-852186

> *Rooms:* include 13 double, 28 twin, 7 family rooms
> *Location:* Central   *Price Range:* ££
> *Restaurant:* à la carte £; table d'hôte £
> *Facilities:* Lift; swimming pool; games room; gardens

Set high above the English Channel, the Victorian-style Royal Hotel has an air of seaside grandeur from days gone by. A holiday hotel, with many facilities to help when the weather is less than kind, it is a happy and relaxed placed to stay, especially for families.

Ventnor is one of the Isle of Wight's premier resorts, on the mild south side of the island. The town itself is hilly, with clifftop walks, and its streets rise in terraces to St Boniface's Down, the highest viewpoint on the island. On one of these terraces stands the Royal Hotel, with its pretty gardens and outdoor swimming pool.

There is a choice of eating place at lunch-time: the foyer buffet, or the formal restaurant. The latter offers a wide-ranging menu and an extra elegance at dinner. There are comfortable lounges, and a relaxing conservatory-style sitting area, and the bar is a haven of peace for a before-dinner or after-dinner drink.

The bedrooms are spacious, and pleasantly furnished, with the emphasis on family accommodation. All have every modern facility, and are in a good international style.

But it is the leisure facilities which make this hotel such a good holiday choice. There are swimming and paddling pools, a children's play area and playroom, an adult games room with table tennis and snooker, and bicycles available for hire.

The Isle of Wight has been called 'Britain in Miniature'. The coast has many sandy beaches, but also features pretty valleys called 'chines', multi-coloured cliffs, and chalk stacks. The interior of the island has historic sites like Carisbrooke Castle and Queen Victoria's summer home at Osborne, and the mainland is only a very short ferry crossing away.

THE GHOST is a Green Lady, whose spectre is often seen on the stairs between the first and second floors of this Victorian building.

Her style of dress suggests that she is somewhat older than the hotel, and seekers after an explanation for this, ever ready to seize upon royal connections, have suggested that she may be linked with King Charles I, who was imprisoned in nearby Carisbrooke Castle.

According to the hotel's owners, religious symbolism used to equate the colour green with faithfulness and 'the resurrection of the just'. So a link with Charles I would reaffirm his right to the throne.

What has all this got to do with a Victorian seaside town? Your guess is as good as mine. Suffice to say that there have been lots of reported sightings of the Green Lady, and that her appearances are always preceded by a noticeable chill in the air. Sometimes the chill is felt without the ghost appearing – and one should hasten to add that this is no reflection on the Royal's excellent central heating.

69 THE ROYAL GEORGE HOTEL

North West

King Street, Knutsford, Cheshire
Telephone: 0565-634151
Fax: 0565-634955

Rooms: include 9 double, 5 twin, 4 family rooms
Location: Central *Price Range:* ££
Restaurant: à la carte £ *Facilities:* Lift

One of the oldest hotels in Cheshire, the Royal George at Knutsford was first established in the fourteenth century. Knutsford itself is an ancient settlement, supposedly named after King Canute, who crossed the river here in the eleventh century. But the charming red brick building of today's Royal George dates back to Georgian times, and was accorded the title 'Royal' after a visit by Queen Victoria who, it sems, was delighted with the hospitality and comfort offered by the hotel.

The lounges and bars are furnished in pretty traditional fabrics, and have a warm and welcoming period atmosphere. There are plenty of antiques to grace the rooms too, and the Cranford Restaurant – named for the novel by Mrs Gaskell, which was set in a town modelled on Knutsford – is cosy with gleaming wood and soft lighting. It serves a steakhouse style menu, with specialities of the day to add an international flavour.

There are 31 bedrooms, all elegantly decorated and featuring Laura Ashley fabrics to contrast a wealth of period detail and antiques. The Queen Victoria Room has an historic four-poster bed, as do the George and Tatton Rooms. The bedrooms have all mod cons and carefully-placed lighting to make tasks like writing or make-up easy.

Knutsford is a pretty town, full of charming old streets. Medieval Chester, with its walls and Roman remains, is only a short drive away, and the lovely stately home of Tatton Park is just outside Knutsford and well worth a visit. Liverpool, with its two cathedrals and Beatles connections as well as its Tate Gallery, is a worthwhile excursion.

THE GHOST is that of Edward Higgins, a former resident of the inn.

During the eighteenth century a noblewoman, Lady Warburton, spent a night at the inn and attracted many admiring glances from her fellow guest. But Edward wasn't after her body – he was after the jewels which she foolishly wore to dinner. For

Edward's profession – which he had failed to mention to his hosts – was that of highwayman.

Next day, he duly relieved Lady Warburton of her diamonds. He got away with his crime, but the forces of law and order were closing in on him and he was captured soon afterwards.

Edward Higgins was hanged in Chester in 1767, but his ghost still hangs around the place which he boldly used as his headquarters, and is still seen occasionally by staff and guests at the Royal George.

70 ST GEORGE HOTEL Northumbria
Tees-side Airport, Darlington, Co. Durham DL2 1RH
Telephone: 0325-332631
Telex: 587623

> *Rooms:* 6 double, 53 twin
> *Location:* Commercial area   *Price Range:* £££
> *Restaurant:* à la carte ££; table d'hôte £

This modern, low-slung building is not just another airport hotel. Its red brick walls, pierced with Georgian-style windows, conceal a very attractive interior furnished in a period style, and with plenty of pleasant places to sit and relax.

Warm wood panels and doors with arched lights let into them add character to the public rooms, and the bar is delightfully furnished with easy chairs and pretty brass and stained-glass details. It serves an excellent range of bar meals for those in a hurry, or travelling with children. The main restaurant is a pretty place to dine, and is decorated in a timeless period style, with light Georgian panelled walls and with elegant drapes. It has a good reputation, and its menu is a mix of local specialities, making the most of fresh local produce, and French cuisine.

The 59 bedrooms are well furnished in restful pale shades, and have all modern amenities. Spacious and comfortable, they are also quiet – something not to be take for granted in an airport hotel. There is an elegant suite with a brass four-poster bed and its own sitting room.

Although the hotel is only 200 yards from the airport terminal, it is a peaceful place, and enjoys open views over the Cleveland Hills and the North Yorkshire Moors. There is a racquets club and leisure centre just across the road.

Yarm, a delightful market town, is only a few miles away, and there is lovely country all around for walking. The historic city of Durham, with its castle and cathedral, is an interesting excursion, and the coastal resorts of Scarborough and Whitby – the latter with its Dracula connections – are only a short drive from the hotel.

THE GHOST is a spirit with a fear of flying. It is believed to be that of an RAF fighter pilot who died in a plane crash in 1951 on the site of what is now Tees-side Airport's St George Hotel. Everyone who has come across the ghost has had something to do with airlines or aeroplanes.

British Midland Airways staff use the hotel for overnight stops, and both pilots and cabin staff have reported spooky experiences there. The most comprehensive report was made by Captain Barney Concannon, who told an airline magazine that he awoke to feel a heavy pressure on both legs during the night, and found that his room had become very cold. Used to issuing orders, Captain Concannon said: 'Using my most authoritative voice, I told the presence to go away – not the actual words, but close enough. The weight immediately left my legs, and the temperature of the room increased.

Although the St George Hotel is relatively new and not the sort of place that one connects with the supernatural, Captain Concannon's experience was far from unique.

An airline steward claims that he was thrown bodily off his bed during the night by an unseen force, and a stewardess says that invisible hands kept opening and closing her bedroom curtains.

Many other guests have complained of flying objects in their rooms, and some have reported shadowy figures. The reports have one thing in common: every one was made by an airline employee.

71 THE SCOLE INN East Anglia
Scole, nr Diss, Norfolk
Telephone: 0379-740481

Rooms: 13 double, 3 twin
Location: Rural   *Price Range:* ££
Restaurant: à la carte ££; table d'hôte £
Facilities: Historic building

A wealthy Norfolk wool merchant, John Peck, built the Scole Inn in 1655, on a crossroads just outside Diss. Today, the inn looks just as it did then: an ornate and unspoiled example of seventeenth-century English architecture made of stout red brick with a gabled roof. An ornate iron sign hangs outside, with the inn's emblem of a white hart figuring prominently. But not as prominently as did the original sign, which stretched like an arch right across the road; made of wood, it cost John Peck more than £1,000 – a fortune in 1655!

For all the changes that have been made to bring the inn up to modern standards of comfort, the travellers of past centuries would still recognise the rooms. And they would certainly recognise the great oak staircase, which shows the marks of a horse's hoofs. Highwayman John Belcher used to show off by galloping up these stairs when he visited the inn in the eighteenth century.

The hotel's bars and restaurants offer old-fashioned charm and historic detail, along with menus ranging from light bar meals to the very best of English cooking, using local ingredients, served in the beautiful Dining Room with its oak furniture and old prints. There are vast open fireplaces with massive lintels, oak beams and panelling, and lots of antiques and period pieces.

The hotel has 16 bedrooms, some in the main house and the remainder in the newly converted Georgian stable block. All are furnished with antiques, and some have historic beds – canopied and draped, with rich mahogany headboards. The sundial room, however, now has a normal bed rather than the original circular bed accommodating 30 sleepers, feet to the centre, a drawing of which is etched on the room's walls. And all the bedrooms have the usual modern amenities.

Located almost in the centre of East Anglia, the Scole Inn is only two miles from the pretty market town of Diss, and 20 miles from the county town of Norwich with its cathedral and excellent shopping. The seaside resorts of Great Yarmouth and Lowestoft, and elegant Aldeburgh, are only an hour away by car.

THE GHOST is that of a wronged woman. Unjustly accused of infidelity, she was murdered by her husband while visiting the inn in the mid-eighteenth century. She has often been seen on the great oak staircase, and in the ground-floor rooms.

Although no-one can put a name to the ghost, it is generally thought that she is Emma, wife of a gentleman staying at the inn in the 1750s. She must have been both pretty and charming, for she attracted a lot of attention from her fellow travellers – especially the notorious highwayman John Belcher.

Belcher, when he was being pursued by the law, used to hide both himself and his horse in the inn's bedrooms. On one such escapade he noticed Emma, and his glances fired her husband's jealousy. The man flew into a rage, refused to listen to her protestations of innocence, and murdered her. Others vouched for Emma's fidelity, but it was too late.

Emma has been reported as a sad pale shape, in long robes, floating down the staircase – her feet not touching the treads scarred by Belcher's horse. She has also been seen in the bars, and at the entrance to the inn.

72 SHIELDHILL
Strathclyde

Quothquan, Biggar, Lanarkshire ML12 6NA, Scotland
Telephone: 0899-20035
Fax: 0899-21092

Rooms: 9 double
Price Range: ££££
Restaurant: prix fixe £
Facilities: Historic building

Location: Rural

Shieldhill

Set well off the beaten track in the Scottish Lowlands is the lovely house of Shieldhill. Built by the Chancellor family in 1199, and in whose keeping it was until 1959, the granite house – with its old Keep extended into Jacobean, and later Georgian, additions – gazes over peaceful meadows set with massive trees and the occasional folly.

Shieldhill was rescued from being a mediocre and run-down hotel in 1988 by American Jack Greenwald and his Scottish partner, Christine Dunstan. Now it is arguably one of the best country house hotels in Britain. Christine's touch is everywhere, especially in the decor using lovely Laura Ashley fabrics. Jack's influence is evident in the cuisine.

The entrance hall, in the old Keep, is flagged and has a secret stairway leading up to the Glencoe room and other suites. The lounge and restaurant are panelled and furnished with rich drapes, and well stocked with newspapers and magazines to browse through in front of the roaring log fires.

The restaurant serves fresh local ingredients, imaginatively used to create a delicious choice of dishes. But if dinner is a gourmet experience, there is a distinct American touch at breakfast – when a hearty steak-and-eggs platter is on the menu.

The spacious bedrooms are all so comfortable that it's hard to tear yourself away; each is individually decorated to suit its style, with vast beds – including four-posters – and designer bathrooms. The Chancellor Suite, also known as the 'honeymoon suite', has a huge whirlpool bath set on a dais and almost large enough to double as a swimming pool.

There is a very friendly atmosphere at Shieldhill, and the young staff are highly attentive. They obviously care about the house, and the welfare of their guests. The result is that everyone feels at home as well as feeling pampered.

Glasgow and Edinburgh are both less than an hour away by car, and the lovely Lowland scenery made famous by Sir Walter Scott is all around.

THE GHOST is of an unnamed daughter of the Chancellor family, who used to live at Shieldhill. During the troubled times of the seventeenth century, when there was a lot of military activity in the Scottish Lowlands, the girl was raped by passing soldiery and became pregnant.

Her horrified family locked her away in what is now the Glencoe Room, where she remained until she gave birth to the child. When the baby was born she wanted to keep it despite the circumstances, but the family would not risk the shame and took it away from her. Then, following a custom of the time, they abandoned it in a field to die.

Cruelly, they chose a spot within sight of the Glencoe Room, and present owners Jack Greenwald and Christine Dunstan will point it out to you if you are interested. They tend to play down the fact that some people – including the plumber who installed the hotel's central heating – have seen the distraught young mother walking through the wall between the Culloden Room and the spectacular honeymoon suite, along what used to be a corridor.

She is also said to pace the flat roof above the honeymoon suite, which bears her family name, at night, searching desperately for her child. There is no access to this bit of roof from the hotel – but I have personal experience of hearing footsteps above my head whilst sleeping in the honeymoon suite: which may be the nearest I've been to seeing a hotel ghost.

73 THE SHIP HOTEL South East England

Monument Green, Weybridge, KT13 8BQ
Telephone: 0932-848364
Fax: 0932-857153

> *Rooms:* include 7 double, 21 twin
> *Location:* Central *Price Range:* £££
> *Restaurant:* à la carte ££; table d'hôte £

When the Ship started life in the early eighteenth century as a coaching inn with strong seafaring connections, its first landlord, John Dryland, paid an annual rent of just one farthing. Nowadays, given its central location in the thriving business town of Weybridge, it is probably worth rather more. But the inn has withstood both

The Ship Hotel

economic pressures and military alarms over the years to offer hospitality to travellers as well as providing a centre for business people.

The hotel is a long, low, white building, still looking today much as it did when John Dryland took over in 1729. Despite his name, Dryland was a seafaring man, and he wanted the Ship to be a sporting venue. The remains of an old cockpit can still be seen there, and a bull-baiting ring occupied what is now the square outside the hotel.

Nowadays, there are no such cruel pastimes. The Ship is a comfortable and characterful hotel, its rooms showing their ancestry with beamed ceilings and Georgian plasterwork. Stylish period furniture makes the bright lounge a restful place to relax, and tapestried furnishings and old prints give the cocktail bar – where the port is, naturally, served in a ship's decanter – an old-fashioned charm.

Wooster's English Country House Restaurant specialises in homely yet dignified traditional cooking, catering both for simple and gourmet tastes. The occasional exotic dish adds spice to the menu.

The hotel's 39 bedrooms are elegantly furnished in period style, with matching drapes and spreads, and have pleasantly subdued lighting. They all have the expected modern amenities. And, for a town-centre hotel, they are surprisingly peaceful.

Convenient for London and Heathrow Airport, Weybridge is an attractive town set in the Surrey hills. The Royal Horticultural Society's spectacular gardens at Wisley are nearby, and Ascot racecourse is an attraction in season. For golfing aficionados there are championship courses at Sunningdale or Wentworth. Windsor Castle and the town's fascinating Royalty and Empire exhibition are only a short drive away, together with the lovely countryside of the Thames Valley.

THE GHOST is that of a man who hanged himself in what is now Room 13.

The suicide took place when the inn was adjoined by a chapel, and it was from the chapel's high beams that the unhappy man hanged himself. Because this had happened on consecrated ground, the chapel was closed and eventually became a billiard hall.

In the early part of this century the roof line was changed and the former chapel was incorporated into the hotel. The area below the chapel room became Room 13.

But no-one will sleep there, and the room has now been bricked off from the inside, although it still has a window: the one in the top right-hand corner of the building as you look at it from the front. Says general manager Rob Hunter: 'If you are ever told there is no room at the inn at The Ship, don't you believe it. There's always a spare bed – if you don't mind sharing with the hotel's longest-staying guest!'

74 STON EASTON PARK   West Country

Ston Easton, nr Bath, Somerset BA3 3DF
Telephone: 0761241-631
Fax: 0761241-377

Rooms: 21 double
Location: Rural   *Price Range:* £££££££
Restaurant: table d'hôte £££
Facilities: Historic building; billiards; croquet; extensive grounds

What does one do with a family home that has become too large for its family? Peter and Christine Smedley had the answer when the handsome Palladian mansion of Ston Easton Park, near Bath, which they purchased 17 years ago, became too big for them: they turned it into a country house hotel.

Although this is a very up-market hotel, the homely atmosphere prevails. And for all the grandeur of the rooms, there is a very comfortable and relaxed ambience. The house itself, on the site of an earlier Tudor mansion, was built by the Hippisley-Coxe family in 1739, and has wonderful panelled and plasterworked rooms, including the Painted Room whose walls still show the decorations of the earlier house. The vast Saloon – which has been described as 'the finest room in Somerset' – the warm Library and the Drawing Room with its lovely views over the valley, are for guests' use, and drinks are served in any corner that a visitor might fancy, direct from the butler's pantry.

The house has 21 guest bedrooms, all of them exquisitely decorated and containing antique furniture and four-poster or other grand beds. There are some imaginative touches, like the bright campaign wardrobes – tent-like structures in fabrics matching the room. And the private bathrooms have been converted from the original eighteenth-century powder-closets. The overall feeling is of great luxury.

But for dinner, guests have to go 'below stairs' to the former servants hall. There, the extensive table d'hote menu includes some distinctly elegant dishes featuring fresh ingredients from the estate.

The estate is on the grand side, too. It has beautiful landscaped gardens by one of the great gardeners, Repton, and include rivers, bridges and a folly. There are woods to wander in, and even the remains of a Victorian curiosity: a huge telescope stand in the paddock. It is possible to arrive by helicopter or to take a hot-air balloon ride in these wonderful grounds.

The Georgian city of Bath is only 11 miles away, and the cathedral city of Wells makes an interesting visit. There is fine countryside all around and the tranquil Somerset villages are pleasant to explore.

THE GHOST is that of a housekeeper, who in the late 1700s murdered one of the maids. She has often been seen wafting through the Ludlow Room, part of her domain while she was working at Ston Easton.

What caused the killing is not clear. Unrequited love or jealousy, perhaps. All that one can say for certain is that the housekeeper, who was undoubtedly of mature years and homely countenance, caught the younger, prettier, still-room maid kissing the estate bailiff. She promptly flew into a rage and attacked the girl, fatally injuring her.

The characters in this drama can still be seen in a picture redolent of the best of television's *Upstairs, Downstairs* sagas. Before the incident the then owners of Ston Easton had a group portrait painted of key members of staff – including the housekeeper, the maid and the bailiff.

Present owners Peter and Christine Smedley will point out the picture to anyone who asks, and it is most revealing. The housekeeper sits stolidly, going over the books with the bailiff. But he appears to be gazing past her and straight at the slender, chintz-clad form of the maid. A scruffier character, the gamekeeper, looks on somewhat apprehensively.

The maid looks rather a tease – perhaps she led the bailiff on, to spite her superior. But her wiles misfired. She died, and the housekeeper – whose fate is not known – still roams the 'downstairs' of the mansion.

However, she knows her place. The house as a whole has no cold spots, and the atmosphere is far from unhappy.

75 THE STRADEY PARK HOTEL
Wales

Furnace, Llanelli, Dyfed SA15 4HA, Wales
Telephone: 0554-758171
Telex: 48521

Rooms: 19 double, 58 twin, 3 family rooms
Location: Central   *Price Range:* ££
Restaurant: à la carte ££; table d'hôte £
Facilities: Lift

An imposing manor house with crenellated roof forms the centre of the Stradey Park Hotel, overlooking Carmarthen Bay and the Gower Peninsula. Although it has been widely extended to provide a range of rooms and facilities with both old and new flavours, the hotel maintains a pleasant and unhurried atmosphere.

The public rooms have many nice pieces of antique furniture, and the restaurant, the Baron's Table, offers a choice of either a carvery menu or a range of international dishes featuring local Welsh specialities. And, for guests' extra amusement, there are Welsh folklore evenings and dinner dances throughout the summer.

Although this is predominantly a business hotel, there are many extras which appeal to holiday guests and families in particular – for example a special children's menu and baby alarm facilities.

The hotel's bedrooms are pleasantly furnished and equipped with all modern amenities. The natural-toned decorative schemes have some innovative finishes.

Stradey Park is only a penalty kick away from the Llanelli Rugby Football Club, one of the most famous in Wales, and within walking distance is the town's great beauty spot, the Swiss Valley. A short drive away are the vast sandy beaches of Burry Port and Cefn Sidan, and the lovely Pembrey Country Park is an unspoilt coastal nature reserve containing more than 500 acres of woodlands, grassy meadows and sand dunes and a vast beach. There is a great deal of industrial heritage in the area – gold mines, coal mines and slate quarries can be visited. And the Brecon Beacons and the Black Mountains are a scenic excursion.

THE GHOST is the figure of a woman, dressed in white, who is seen quite often in the older parts of the building.

A Georgian manor house formed the main part of this hotel, and the suggestion is that the White Lady was a former resident – perhaps a spinster daughter – of the house.

There have been very recent sightings by both staff and guests, who say that the ghost has a distinctly Dickensian appearance. Apart from that, there are no clues to her identify or to her origins.

76 THE SUFFOLK HOTEL   East Anglia

38 Buttermarket, Bury St Edmunds, Suffolk IP33 1DL
Telephone: 0284-753995
Fax: 0284-750973

Rooms: include 14 double, 11 twin
Location: Central   *Price Range:* ££
Restaurant: The Tower Restaurant (international) à la carte ££; table d'hôte £; The Suffolk Pantry (coffee shop) £

The Suffolk Hotel

In the centre of the market town of Bury St Edmunds, near the old Abbey, there once was an inn known as The Greyhound – owned by the Abbey and, in the sixteenth century, a focus for townspeople and visitors. Modernised in Georgian times and renamed The Suffolk, it is now a pleasant hotel – and it is still a popular meeting place.

Bury is almost in the centre of East Anglia, and has grown from a quiet backwater into a significant business hub. But the Suffolk Hotel preserves an old-world restraint and calm behind its plastered facade. The Tower Restaurant, with decor reminiscent of olde England, has a range of dishes reflecting the best of French and English cooking. The coffee shop, the Suffolk Pantry, offers light meals and drinks throughout the day, amid the pine dressers and dried flowers of a country kitchen-style decor. The Viking Bar is a cosy meeting place.

The Suffolk has 33 bedrooms, all with the usual modern amenities and pleasantly furnished to a good international standard. Rooms are spacious, and have co-ordinated pastel colour schemes.

The remains of Bury's Abbey, dating back to the tenth century, are now filled with lovely gardens, and the fourteenth-century gateway is especially beautiful. Queen Mary Tudor was buried here. There is a delightful Queen Anne house, dated 1711, in the town, containing a museum of clocks and watches, and the streets are lined with interesting buildings, including one of the smallest pubs in Britain.

The Suffolk coast, with its sandy beaches, is less than an hour away, and the lovely old 'wool towns', their medieval and thatched buildings half-hidden beside massive churches paid for by the local wool industry, are all around.

THE GHOST is that of a monk, who has been on the bottle! In fact, the hotel has a barrel-load of spectral monks – and the whole bevy of them have been on the bevvy!

During the sixteenth century the Suffolk belonged to the Abbey of Bury St Edmunds, and its cellars were linked to the Abbey by underground tunnels. There can be little doubt that the monks, thirsty after a day's devotions, used to pop along these tunnels in search of a little liquid refreshment.

And they are still at it! According to the hotel's management, it is not unusual for twentieth-century visitors to come across their forbears who, sad to say, are usually the worse for drink. One carousing monk, flagon in hand, has even been known to stray beyond the confines of the building into the Buttermarket outside – for all the world like a present-day lager lout.

But the similarity ends there. The spectral soaks are a merry bunch, who do no harm and vanish just as suddenly as they appear. The ghost seen most frequently is a monk in one of the old tunnels, and if you need to share the drinking habits of the rest of them before seeing them... well, no doubt the hotel bar will be happy to accommodate you.

77 SUNLAWS HOUSE   Lowlands

Kelso, Roxburghshire, Scotland TD5 8JZ
Telephone: 05735-331
Telex: 728147

Rooms: include 19 double, 6 twin
Location: Rural   *Price Range:* £££
Restaurant: à la carte ££; table d'hôte £
Facilities: Historic building; extensive grounds

For 500 years, this imposing residence was a family house on the Duke of Roxburghe's estate near Kelso. Now the Duke has turned it into an hotel, that family feeling persists.

Set in 200 acres of garden and woodland, with the river Teviot running through its grounds, Sunlaws has been the scene of many skirmishes between the English and the Scots since the fifteenth century. Bonnie Prince Charlie stayed at Sunlaws in November 1745, while leading the Jacobite rebellion, and there is still a white rose bush in the grounds, which is a descendant of one that the Prince planted to commemorate his visit. But it is a battleground no longer. Looking out of the front door today, it is hard to imagine anything but peace at Sunlaws.

The entrance hall to this, one of the nicest hotels in Britain, contains a vast fireplace where log fires blaze merrily in season. Off the hall is the very cosy Library Bar where the ranks of malt whiskies offer an alternative method of getting warm. It is quite likely that visitors will also find His Grace doing reception duty: for he is very much a 'hands-on' proprietor.

The Georgian restaurant, with its elegant plasterwork panels, prides itself on the use of local ingredients from the Duke's forests and fish from his stretch of the Teviot.

The 27 bedrooms range from the modern and extremely well-equipped, in the Stable block, to the historic and equally comfortable in the main house. The latter offer four-poster beds and tented ceilings, elegant and very exclusive soft furnishings, and ducal antiques and family portraits everywhere.

There is a lounge overlooking the gardens, and a conservatory which not only furnishes plants and flowers for the house but is also a pretty spot for afternoon tea or a pre-dinner cocktail.

Kelso is in Scott Country, and the author's home at Abbotsford is worth a visit. The Duke of Roxburghe is a neighbour at Floors Castle, which can also be visited and where hotel guests get a special welcome. Alnwick, a pretty Northumberland border market town with a castle full of antiquities, is not far away, and Holy Island is also within easy reach.

THE GHOST is that of a Second World War soldier, probably an Italian prisoner. Sunlaws was used as an internment centre for PoWs during the 1940s, and workmen in the attics – which are not used nowadays – have seen a gaunt, uniformed figure. The suggestion seems to be that the attic was used as, or was above, the camp's medical centre – so perhaps the soldier was a sad inmate longing for the home he never saw again.

But the night porter claims that Sunlaws also has another ghost. He has often seen the misty figure of a woman drifting dreamily around the lobby at the bottom of the main staircase. She then moves across the lounge and disappears somewhere in the region of the conservatory.

Other staff on duty late at night have witnessed the phenomenon, which seems to be confined to the wee small hours. But no guests have ever reported anything odd.

78 THE SWAN HOTEL North West
Bucklow Hill, Knutsford, Cheshire WA16 6RD
Telephone: 0565-830295
Telex: 66691

Rooms: include 24 double, 15 twin, 11 family rooms
Location: Rural *Price Range:* ££
Restaurant: à la carte ££; table d'hôte £
Facilities: Gardens

The village of Bucklow Hill, just outside the little Cheshire town of Knutsford, has had a rougher passage than most through history, and always seemed to be at the heart of such events as the Civil War.

But the old Swan Hotel has survived it all. Once a monastery, the long, low building still shows traces of its origins, with thick walls, lots of oak beams and unexpected nooks and crannies, and windows in improbable places.

The Swan was an important staging post on the journey to Manchester, and it retains its reputation for hospitality. The atmosphere is peaceful, comfortable and elegant, and the attentive staff are always on hand to make a visitor's stay more pleasant.

The lounges and bar, with their oak beams and panelling, are full of period furniture and the restaurant – which is on several levels – is rich with matching drapes and lamps and carved wood. The cuisine is international in flavour, but the breakfasts are in true Cheshire tradition: immense and hearty. The chef has a speciality month from time to time, when the menu takes on a seasonal flavour – seafood or game, for example.

There are 70 bedrooms, all very well fitted and with elegant furnishings in pastel tones in keeping with each room's atmosphere. Some have whirlpool spa baths, and there are three rooms with beautiful old carved and inlaid four-poster beds. Period details abounds, like old porcelain telephone handsets and brass lamps.

Apart from Knutsford, which retains a good deal of its early Victorian market town charm, the Swan is only 30 minutes' drive from Manchester, with its wealth of museums and the newly popular Granada TV Studios to visit. Chester, with its medieval walls and Roman remains, also has lovely shops in the Rows.

THE GHOST is that of Lady Combermere. But on this occasion the 'lady' is a horse.

In 1898 the then owner of The Swan, Thomas Ackerley, bought a famous trotting mare called Lady Combermere, which had set a record by covering 20 miles in less than an hour. The fleet-footed filly was his pride and joy, and when she died in 1911, at the grand old age of 26, she was duly given a final resting place within the hotel grounds. Her body still lies buried, under an ornate headstone, outside what is now the bedroom quadrangle. One bit of her still above ground is her hooves, which Thomas Ackerley had silver-plated and which still grace the hotel bar.

Silver-plated they may be, but they seem reluctant to be still. Over the years, many members of staff and guests have reported hearing the sound of phantom hooves trotting around the car park, whilst others have seen a phantom horse in the same area. A few have even claimed that the phantom horse came complete with headless rider.

Manager Richard Grey hasn't seen The Lady himself despite having been at the hotel for six years, but he says, mysteriously: 'There was one occasion when I thought something strange was happening'. However, Mr Grey is an honest soul, for he adds: 'I put that down to a surfeit of good food, fine wine and port'.

79 THE TALBOT HOTEL   East Midlands
New Street, Oundle, nr Peterborough, Northamptonshire PE8 4EA
Telephone: 0832-273621
Fax: 0832-274545

> *Rooms:* include 25 double, 9 twin
> *Location:* Central   *Price Range:* £££
> *Restaurant:* à la carte ££; table d'hôte £

Fotheringhay Castle's loss is Oundle's gain, because the lovely old inn in the centre of Oundle, the Talbot, was built from materials taken from nearby Fotheringhay after its destruction by the son of Mary, Queen of Scots, as revenge for her execution.

Built in 1626, when it replaced an older inn, the Talbot has transomed windows and gables topped with stone balls to decorate its grey stone walls. The very imposing Tudor staircase is that down which Mary often walked in her imprisonment and on her way to her eventual execution in 1587; it was transplanted to the Talbot as the inn was being constructed.

Today, the Talbot has kept many of its original features, and the restaurant especially boasts fine old beams. The menu of good English cooking is complemented by the light meals served at lunch-time in the Lounge Bar, with its open log fire, and the more intimate Snug. The chefs make a speciality of 'food festivals' from time to time, when the menus take on the flavour of some far-flung (or not so far-flung) corner of the globe.

The hotel's 39 bedrooms are decorated in a classic international style, and most are newly refurbished with canopied beds and elegant drapes. All have modern amenities, and there are four suites which provide ample space for a family.

Oundle is a charming town of historic stone houses, a beautiful church, and of course its public school. The River Nene runs close to the hotel, so boating and fishing can be added to the town's recreational possibilities.

The cathedral cities of Ely and Peterborough are only a short drive away, and the ancient villages of Fotheringhay, Dene and Cotterstock are all worth seeing. Burghley House, with its art treasures and horse trials, is nearby and Barnwell Castle, the home of the Duke and Duchess of Gloucester, is open to visitors.

THE GHOST is the spirit of Mary, Queen of Scots. Although the Talbot was built about 40 years after her execution in 1587, stonework from Fotheringhay Castle – where she was imprisoned before her death – was used in its construction. And the castle's staircase was moved to the Talbot in its entirety.

Along with the staircase came the ghost. Mary, Queen of Scots, must have walked up and down it endlessly in the days before she was beheaded – and her spirit walks up and down it still. No: she does not have her head tucked underneath her arm. On the contrary, she is whole, highly visible and easily recognisable from her portraits. In fact she is one of Britain's best-known and most widely documented ghosts, and sightings of her in the hotel are very frequent.

Whilst the royal ghost confines her appearances to the staircase, however, the Talbot has another mystery which seems to encompass the entire building. At odd times, in almost any corner of the building, there may be heard the sound of a woman wailing, sobbing, and sometimes singing. Mysterious footsteps are also heard – yet there is never any obvious explanation for any of these sounds.

The hotel management's theory is that the sounds are made by the spirit of one of Mary, Queen of Scots' four maids – who, incidentally, were all called Mary – still mourning for her mistress.

80 TIBBIE SHIELS INN   Lowlands
St Mary's Loch, Selkirkshire, Scotland
Telephone: 0750-42231

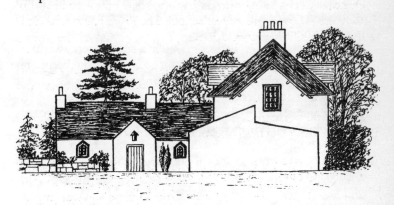

Rooms: 2 double, 2 twin
Location: Rural
Restaurant: à la carte £
Facilities: Fishing

Price Range: £

Tibbie Shiels Inn

This old inn, once just a but-and-ben housing both humans and animals in its two rooms, is now a cosy little hotel on the edge of St Mary's Loch, in the Scottish Lowlands.

Named after a doughty landlady who ran it in the nineteenth century, the inn once served local whisky to local author Sir Walter Scott, who used to sit at the fireside with landlady Tibbie Shiels. The old but-and-ben has been extended several times over the years, and the architectural mix has provided plenty of comfortable corners in which to relax. Present owners John ('Jack') Brown and his wife Jill are eager to restore some of the original features removed by previous owners – but the bar, in one half of the original building, still looks as it did in Tibbie's day, with polished wood and lots of gleaming brass pots.

The original beams are still in evidence, both in the bar and in the old dining-room which was Tibbie's kitchen. The newer dining-room overlooks the loch. In both dining rooms the meals are quite excellent value, and the range of dishes includes venison and other game from local estates. Jill Brown prides herself on her menu, which changes weekly to make the most of fresh local ingredients.

The lounge, a Victorian addition to the hotel, is simply furnished, comfortable, and has commanding views over the hills and the loch from its wide windows.

The inn has four guest bedrooms, all in a single-storey addition which makes the hotel a good place for older folk. The bedrooms are very homely and comfortable, sharing bathrooms, and have panelled walls decorated in pastel shades.

Fishing is available in the hotel's own stretch of loch. Glasgow and Edinburgh – with their shopping, museums and entertainments – are both within easy reach and the Lowlands, about which Sir Walter Scott wrote so much, are all around for walkers and naturalists to enjoy.

THE GHOST is that of Tibbie herself, the inn's landlady in the nineteenth century. She made the inn a popular stopover for sportsmen and travellers and after her death in 1898, at the age of 94, she seemed unable to leave the place. She is often to be felt at her own fireside, tapping guests on the shoulder if they don't leave room for her by the hearth in what is now the old dining-room.

It was Tibbie who turned the family's old farmhouse into an inn after being widowed. She managed to squeeze in up to 35 guests overnight. Today the inn, with far more space, accommodates only eight. But she particularly enjoyed a wee dram at the fireside with locals and regulars, like Sir Walter Scott.

In the crush, she used to have to elbow people aside to reach her favourite chair. Today guests at the inn often report a nudge on their shoulder when no-one is around, and provided they move slightly away from the fire nothing else befalls them. But anyone who ignores Tibbie's warning does so at their peril: she has been known to hurl fire-irons across the room in a fit of pique!

Present owners Jack and Jill Brown have not met Tibbie in their four years of occupancy. But they have met a dog, which has been 'seen' in the bar when no dogs are anywhere to be found. Locals say it is the spectre of a hound belonging to the inn's then owner some 80 years ago. He left it tied up in the room while he went to Ettrick on business, but he collapsed and died while he was away and the dog, tied up alone, died of starvation before being discovered.

And some women guests have felt reluctant to visit the toilet on dark winter nights. They say to have seen a shadowy shape sitting on the landing outside the cloakroom, and claim that it is Tibbie. If it is, she must be a very agile ghost: the cloakroom is in the newer part of the inn, and if Tibbie was alive and sitting where she has been spied, she would be halfway up a tree!

[81] TURNBERRY HOTEL Strathclyde

Turnberry, Ayrshire KA26 9LT, Scotland
Telephone: 0655-31000
Fax: 0655-31706

> *Rooms:* include 15 double, 99 twin
> *Location:* Rural *Price Range:* £££££
> *Restaurant:* à la carte ££; table d'hôte ££
> *Facilities:* Golf and other sports facilities; leisure club; extensive grounds

Turnberry Hotel

Long established as a golfer's paradise, the Turnberry Hotel on the Firth of Clyde was originally part of the huge estates of the Marquis of Ailsa. In Victorian times, with an eye to the future, the Marquis went into partnership with the Glasgow and South Western Railway to develop the estate for golf, and to build a first-class hotel to accommodate players. By 1907, the championship courses had a worldwide reputation.

Today, the hotel is as it was, full of mellow wood panelling and carved plasterwork ceilings. It has a warm and intimate atmosphere for a property of its size, and many guests return time and again for holidays on this lovely stretch of coast, not to mention the many sporting opportunities the 360-acre estate affords.

The entrance hall and adjoining lounge have a turn-of-the-century elegance, with palms and brass chandeliers. Tea taken on the terrace with the sun setting behind the huge rock of Ailsa Craig and the island of Arran is a delightful experience, but to dine in the sumptuous Turnberry Restaurant is even more magical. Not only does the dining-room command the most superb views, but the pillared and alcoved room under an ornate ceiling has a very impressive ambience. The menu is equally impressive, with the best of Scottish ingredients and dishes alongside international gourmet cuisine.

The hotel's 115 bedrooms range from the luxurious to the downright sumptuous, with canopied beds and a four-poster bed with tartan drapes, as well as modern twin beds. All the bedrooms are very comfortable and spacious, and the grand Ocean View Suite has its own terrace.

There will shortly be a new leisure centre on the estate to round out the leisure facilities on offer: golf, of course; croquet; tennis; fishing; and shooting. The city of Glasgow and the scenic Scottish Lowlands are within easy reach, and a trip to Arran or one of its neighbouring islands should not be missed.

THE GHOST is a series of mysterious noises recollecting a brief period in the hotel's history. In a wing of the hotel which is used as staff quarters, there can often be heard the unmistakeable sounds of an old hospital.

The hotel was used for military purposes in both World Wars.

During the Second World War, the staff wing incorporated a medical centre, complete with operating theatre. Since then, staff staying in this wing have often reported waking to hear the sounds of a rubber-wheeled hospital trolley passing down a rubber-floored corridor and through rubber-edged doors – just as in the wartime hospital. But when the staff looked out to see what was causing the noises, all they saw was the normal, bright, staff-wing furnishings, and no-one in sight.

The sounds, reported as recently as the 1970s, were so clear to many who experienced them that it seemed impossible that nothing could be seen. Some susceptible people, however, have reported smelling a mixture of disinfectant and rubber, the odour typical of old-fashioned medical establishments. And some have found the experience unexpectedly harrowing.

But guests need not worry: the wing is not a part of the hotel which they are likely to visit during their stay, and nothing at all odd has been experienced anywhere else in the building.

82 TYLNEY HALL

South of England

Rotherwick, nr Hook, Hampshire RG27 9AJ
Telephone: 025672-4881
Fax: 025672-8141

Rooms: 91 double/twin
Location: Rural   *Price Range:* £££
Restaurant: à la carte ££; table d'hôte £
Facilities: Historic building; swimming pools; snooker; tennis; croquet; golf; extensive grounds

Tylney Hall, a lovely red-brick mansion in the Queen Anne style, is younger than it looks: it is a turn-of-the century building, created on the site of earlier mansions by Sir Lionel Phillips, who bought the vast estate for just £77,000 in 1898.

The house has many features mirroring the Queen Anne period. The Smoking Room ceiling is a copy of a sixteenth-century model; and the Great Hall, with its Italian walnut panelling, has a stone

Tylney Hall

fireplace and ceiling brought from a Renaissance palace in Florence, and installed at Tylney at great expense.

Today, Tylney Hall is a country house hotel in the grand manner. There guests will find peace, space and elegantly unobtrusive service. The restaurant, with its garden views and glass-domed ceiling, serves a menu of haute cuisine favourites. The Library Bar is a very cosy place for a before- or after-dinner drink, and the drawing-rooms are extremely comfortably furnished with period and antique furniture.

The Hall has 91 guest bedrooms. Some are modern, in wings converted from the old Coach House and other outbuildings; the rooms in the main house are full of historic beds with canopies and drapes from the ceiling, and there is a pretty four-poster-bedded suite. All the bedrooms are lavishly furnished, and have every modern amenity alongside the antiques.

The Hall's vast grounds have tennis courts, an outdoor pool, and lovely gardens and woodlands. There is a traditionally-styled billiard-room, and an indoor leisure centre including whirlpool spa.

But if guests are tempted to go farther afield, there is golf on an adjacent course, and the lovely Hampshire villages are all around to make interesting excursions. The south coast, with its sailing centres on the Hamble, is nearby, and the cities of Portsmouth and Southampton are only a short drive away.

THE GHOST is that of a coach drawn by black horses, which dashes noiselessly into the yard beside the hotel, now the car park.

Villagers have often reported seeing the coach, generally in the dead of winter as well as in the dead of night. The somewhat vague legend attached to the story seems to indicate that the coach is travelling an old road which bypassed the earlier hall. This earlier building was demolished in the late eighteenth century by the then owner, who was greedy for the profits to be made from timber on the estate. But there were legal complications, and the only way he could get his hands on the money from the thick forests that then surrounded the hall was to invoke an ill-worded clause in the entail documents, which allowed him to demolish the hall – and fell the forests too.

Whether the coach and horses are in some way a protest against this vandalism is not known. But, especially on New Year's Eve, local people keep their eyes open for the phantom coach and six black horses.

83 WESTON MANOR HOTEL

Thames & Chilterns

Weston-on-the-Green, Oxfordshire OX6 9QL
Telephone: 0869-50621
Fax: 08621-50901

Rooms: include 22 double, 13 twin
Location: Rural   *Price range:* £££
Restaurant: à la carte ££; table d'hôte £
Facilities: Historic building; swimming pool; croquet; squash; extensive grounds

The Normans, newly arrived after the Conquest, took over the lands of Weston Manor from the former owners, and in turn gave it to the Church. As an Abbey, the house survived until the Dissolution of the Monasteries in Tudor times, when the Norreys and Bertie families – as Earls of Berkshire and Abington – made the house the grand building it is today. They cherished it for more than 300 years, and subsequent owners have loved it, too. Now it is a superb moated manor house hotel, owned by Dudley Osborn.

There are still remnants of the Abbey to be found in the Baron's Hall dining-room and adjacent chapel, the latter now used as a small dining-room. With its oak-beamed and panelled interior gleaming with silver and lit candles, the Baron's Hall offers classic dishes based on fresh local produce and fine wines. Diners are surrounded by history: an Abbot's bailiff held court here in the sixteenth century, and there is an archer's loop in the wall in case of attack. A faded ancient fresco can be seen above the fireplace.

The Georgian drawing-room is an elegant and comfortable place to relax in at any time of the day.

There are 37 bedrooms, some in the newly converted stable block, and some in the tithe barn known as Rupert's Cottage. The latter is named after the Cavalier prince who daringly escaped from his Roundhead pursuers by dressing in a maid's clothes after the battle of Weston in 1643. The bedrooms in the main house are richly furnished with antiques and four-poster beds, and all possible conveniences. The principal room, known as the Tudor Room, is oak panelled, has a vast fireplace, and is extremely cosy.

The gardens are beautifully landscaped, and contain a swimming pool and croquet lawn. There is also a squash court in the stable block. Dudley Osborn's hotel is such a relaxing and comfortable experience that visitors may be reluctant to go out into the surrounding country, but interesting places to visit nearby include Oxford, Blenheim Palace, Woodstock, and Stratford-upon-Avon with its Shakespeare connections.

THE GHOST is that of 'Mad Maude', a pretty young nun who was burned at the stake outside Weston Manor in the 1400s, when it was a monastery. She had been caught indulging in some distinctly irreligious activities with the monks.

Still wearing her blue habit, she walks the corridors around Room 7, which is known as the Tudor Room and contains a big four-poster bed. She has also been known to walk through the room: one recent guest awoke to find the wimpled figure leaning over him and thought for a moment that it was his wife – until he realised that she was still asleep beside him.

Another version of the 'Mad Maude' legend is that she was a simple dairymaid, who was pushed to her death from the tower and who left an immovable bloodstain on the floorboards below. The intention was to silence her, because her clothes were being used to disguise Prince Rupert, the younger brother of King Charles I, as he fled from his Roundhead pursuers during the Civil War.

And in the 1980s, this story was given added credence by the then hotel manageress, who reported seeing the apparition of a handsome young man, dressed as a Cavalier and with his hair in ringlets, sitting in the entrance hall and drinking from a goblet. Prince Rupert himself, perhaps, reliving his successful escape from the hotel when it was a private house.

A more tangible Civil War link was found on the manor's estate in Victorian times, when a windmill kept falling down and was discovered to have been erected on the site of a Royalist burial ground – presumably the final resting place of victims of the Battle of Weston in 1643.

Going back to the ghosts, perhaps both nun and dairymaid haunt the hotel, for the sound of female laughter is often heard echoing though the building. And, to complete its collection of strange happenings, Weston Manor can also lay claim to a spectral coach which comes through the yard at the rear of the house and then vanishes. A gardener from the local village who worked in the grounds from the 1960s right up until 1983 saw it so often that he would not risk crossing its route and always took the long way round the yard.

84 THE WHITE HORSE HOTEL

South of England

Market Place, Romsey, Hampshire SO51 8ZJ
Telephone: 0794-512431
Fax: 0794-517485

Rooms: include 17 double, 7 twin
Location: Central   *Price Range:* £££
Restaurant: à la carte £; table d'hôte £

Hidden behind a tall white Georgian frontage in the Hampshire town of Romsey is an hotel with a heart of oak. For the interior of the White Horse Hotel, in the town's centre, is a maze of beautifully preserved beams and open studwork, dating back to the hotel's origins in the sixteenth century.

The lounge, with its open fire with massive lintel and mellow bare brickwork, is furnished in keeping with its atmosphere, and antiques – including a spinning wheel – stand below heraldic shields which line the walls. The Elizabethan Lounge is part of the older building, and its wall is pierced with the original narrow windows which now look on to the corridor extending it to meet the Georgian frontage. It is a very intimate spot, and very peaceful. The hotel's past occupants have left their mark in the vestiges of an old minstrels' gallery and wall paintings dating back to Tudor times.

Manton's Restaurant, in the hotel's Lucella Dixon Room, is classic both in its decor and its dishes, and the adjoining Courtyard Bar offers light meals too, especially attractive in summer when there are tables outside in the old inn yard. The bar specialises in traditional beers in another link with the building's history.

The White Horse has 33 elegantly furnished bedrooms, each with a different toning colour scheme and matched fabrics, and all amenities. And children are very welcome – the hotel's family-sized rooms are generously proportioned and there are special menus for children as well as a baby-listening service.

Romsey grew up on the banks of the River Test, and alongside a tenth-century Abbey. Just a short walk from the hotel is Broadlands,

The White Horse Hotel

home of the Mountbatten family and once the home of Lord Palmerston, one of Queen Victoria's forceful Prime Ministers. The New Forest is on the doorstep, as is the sailing centre of Bucklers Hard. Beaulieu, with its motor museum, is an interesting excursion.

THE GHOST is that of a stable boy, whose spirit still clatters noisily around in his workplace which has long since been incorporated into the hotel buildings.

The young ostler was employed in the stables of the original coaching inn in Elizabethan times, and died there mysteriously and violently. The popular theory is that he and his larger workmates got into a fight over a gambling debt.

Since then, the scene of his death has also been the scene of many mysterious happenings. Unaccountable noises are heard, items move of their own accord, and things really do go bump in the night. Guests and staff report the feeling of a half-seen figure passing on the periphery of their vision – but when they turn to look there is nobody there.

Mysterious they may be, but these experiences are also extraordinarily light-hearted. One gets the feeling that the young ostler is merely still indulging in his boyish pranks.

REGIONAL MAPS

Map 1

Map 3

MAP 4

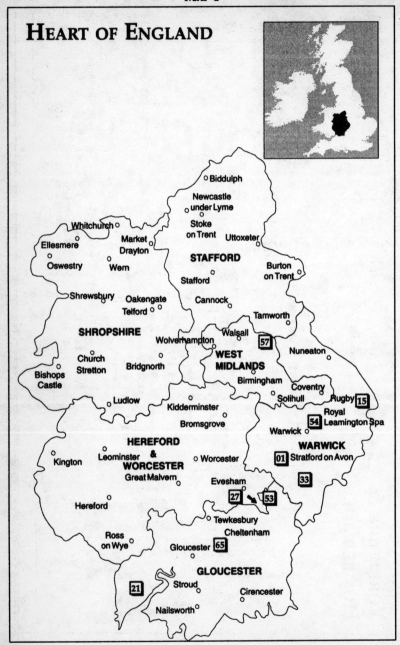

Map 5

East Midlands

Map 6

Map 7

East Anglia

MAP 8

WEST COUNTRY

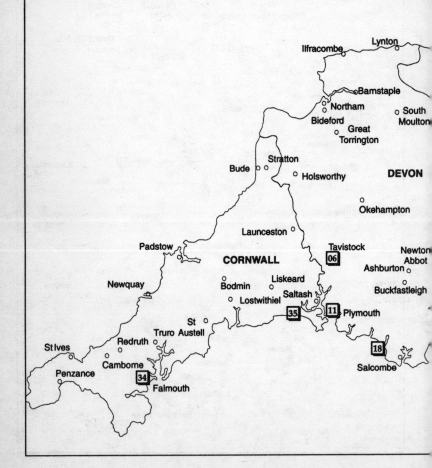

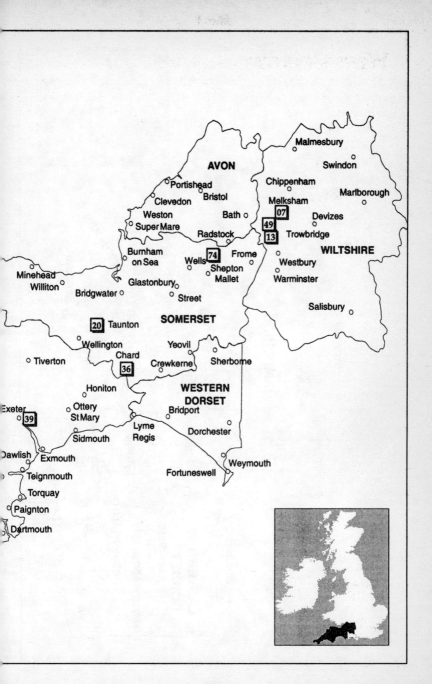

Map 9

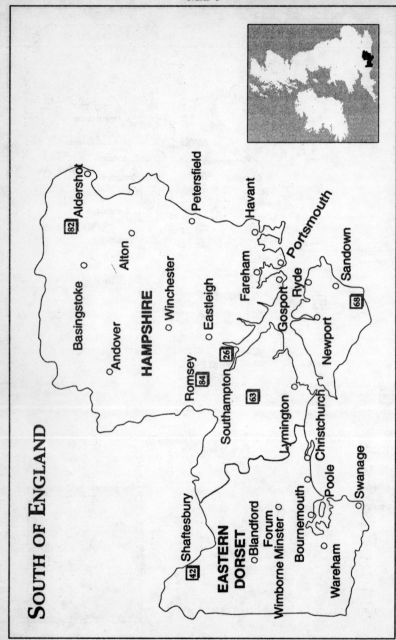

MAP 10

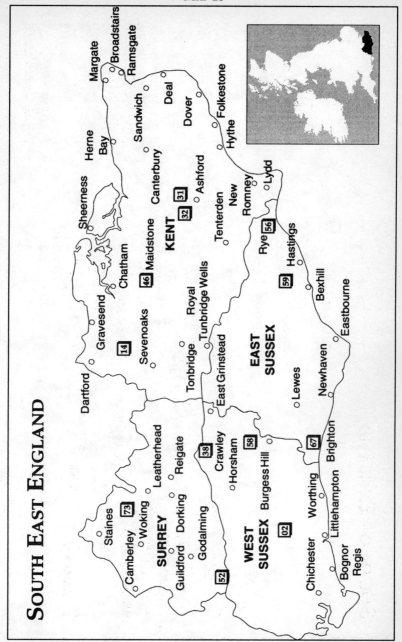

Map 11

Tayside & Grampian

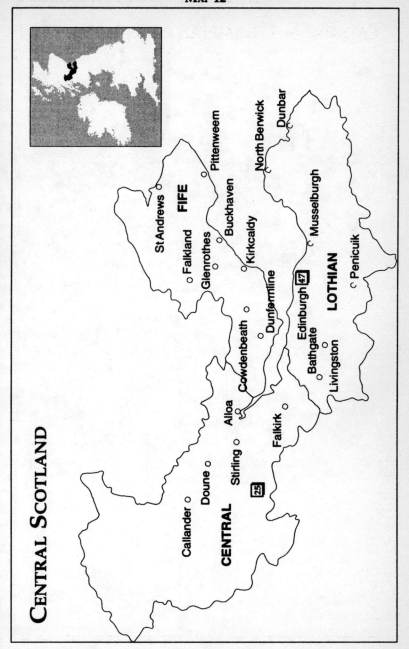

Map 13

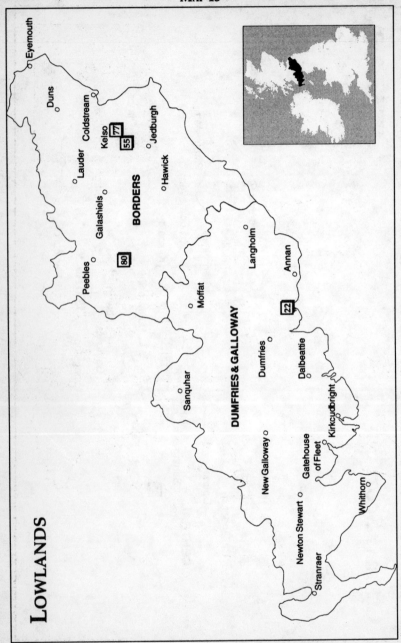

MAP 14

STRATHCLYDE

Map 15

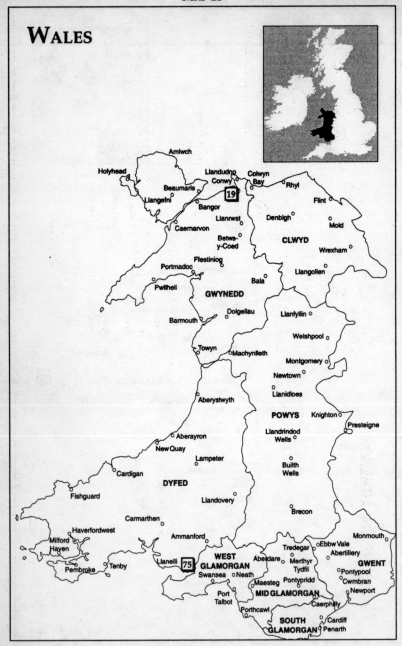

Map 16

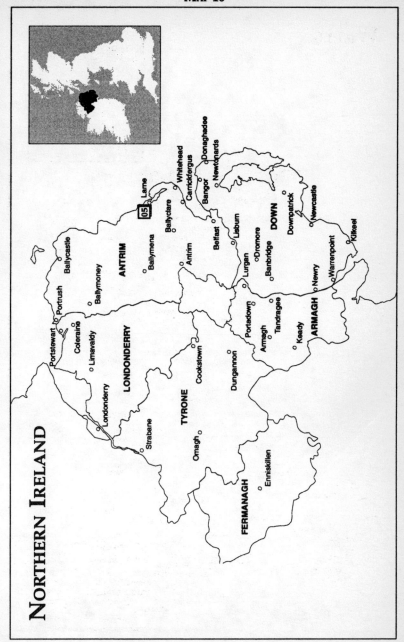

Alphabetical Index of Hotels

The bold figures indicate the map number showing the location of each hotel within its region. A regional index of hotels is given on page 184.

01 *Alveston Manor*, Stratford-upon-Avon, Warwickshire **4**, 1
02 *Amberley Castle*, Amberley, West Sussex **10**, 2
03 *Angel & Royal Hotel, The*, Grantham, Lincolnshire **5**, 5
04 *Atholl Palace*, Pitlochry, Perthshire **11**, 6
05 *Ballygally Castle*, Ballygally, Co. Antrim **16**, 8
06 *Bedford Hotel, The*, Tavistock, Devon **8**, 10
07 *Beechfield House*, Melksham, Wiltshire **8**, 12
08 *Bell Hotel, The*, Thetford, Norfolk **7**, 14
09 *Berystede, The*, Sunninghill, Berkshire **6**, 16
10 *Black Swan Hotel, The*, Helmsley, Yorkshire **3**, 18
11 *Boringdon Hall*, Plympton, Devon **8**, 20
12 *Bosworth Hall*, Market Bosworth, Leicestershire **5**, 22
13 *Bradford Old Windmill*, Bradford-on-Avon, Wiltshire **8**, 24
14 *Brandshatch Place*, Fawkham, Kent **10**, 26
15 *Brownsover Hall*, Rugby, Warwickshire **4**, 28
16 *Bull Hotel, The*, Peterborough, Cambridgeshire **7**, 30
17 *Bull Hotel, The*, Long Melford, Suffolk **7**, 33
18 *Burgh Island*, Bigbury-on-Sea, Devon **8**, 35
19 *Castle Hotel, The*, Conwy, Gwynedd **15**, 37
20 *Castle Hotel, The*, Taunton, Somerset **8**, 39
21 *Clearwell Castle*, Royal Forest of Dean, Gloucestershire **4**, 41
22 *Comlongon Castle*, Clarencefield, Dumfries **13**, 43
23 *Crayke Castle*, Crayke, North Yorkshire **3**, 46
24 *Crown Hotel and Posting House, The*, Bawtry, Yorkshire **3**, 47
25 *Culcreuch Castle*, Fintry, Stirlingshire **12**, 49
26 *Dolphin Hotel, The*, Southampton, Hampshire **10**, 52
27 *Dormy House Hotel*, Willersley Hill, Worcestershire **4**, 53
28 *Duke's Head, The*, King's Lynn, Norfolk **7**, 55
29 *Dunkenhalgh Hotel*, Clayton-le-Moors, Lancashire **2**, 57
30 *Dweldapilton Hall Hotel*, Appleton-le-Moors, Yorkshire **3**, 59
31 *Eastwell Manor*, Boughton Aluph, Kent **10**, 61
32 *Elvey Farm*, Pluckley, Kent **10**, 62
33 *Ettington Park Hotel*, Alderminster, Warwickshire **4**, 64

34 *Falmouth Hotel, The*, Falmouth, Cornwall **8**, 66
35 *Finnygook Inn, The*, Crafthole, Cornwall **8**, 68
36 *Forde Abbey*, Chard, Somerset **8**, 70
37 *Gairnshiel Lodge*, Ballater, Aberdeenshire **11**, 72
38 *George Hotel, The*, Crawley, Sussex **10**, 74
39 *Globe Hotel, The*, Topsham, Devon **8**, 76
40 *Golden Lion, The*, St Ives, Cambridgeshire **7**, 78
41 *Grand Hotel, The*, Lincoln, Lincolnshire **5**, 80
42 *Grosvenor Hotel, The*, Shaftesbury, Dorset **9**, 82
43 *Haycock Hotel, The*, Peterborough, Cambridgeshire **7**, 83
44 *Hintlesham Hall*, Hintlesham, Suffolk **7**, 86
45 *Knights Hill Hotel, The*, South Wootton, Norfolk **7**, 88
46 *Larkfield Priory Hotel*, Larkfield, Kent **10**, 89
47 *Learmonth Hotel, The*, Edinburgh **12**, 91
48 *Lee Wood Hotel*, Buxton, Derbyshire **5**, 92
49 *Leigh Park Hotel*, Bradford-on-Avon, Wiltshire **8**, 94
50 *Lord Crewe Arms, The*, Blanchland, County Durham **1**, 95
51 *Lumley Castle*, Chester-le-Street, County Durham **1**, 97
52 *Lythe Hill Hotel*, Haslemere, Surrey **10**, 99
53 *Malt House, The*, Chipping Campden, Gloucestershire **4**, 102
54 *Manor House Hotel, The*, Royal Leamington Spa, Warwickshire **4**, 103
55 *Marlfield House*, Kelso, Roxburghshire **13**, 105
56 *Mermaid Hotel, The*, Rye, Sussex **10**, 107
57 *New Hall*, Sutton Coldfield, Warwickshire **4**, 109
58 *Ockenden Manor*, Cuckfield, Sussex **10**, 111
59 *Old Deanery, The*, Battle, East Sussex **10**, 113
60 *Old Swan Hotel, The*, Harrogate, North Yorkshire **3**, 116
61 *Pannanich Wells Hotel*, Ballater, Royal Deeside **11**, 118
62 *Park International Hotel, The*, Leicester, Leicestershire **5**, 120
63 *Parkhill Hotel*, Lyndhurst, Hampshire **9**, 122
64 *Ponden Hall*, Stanbury, West Yorkshire **3**, 123
65 *Prestbury House Hotel*, Prestbury, Gloucestershire **4**, 125
66 *Redworth Hall*, Redworth, County Durham **1**, 127
67 *Regency Hotel, The*, Brighton, Sussex **10**, 129
68 *Royal Hotel, The*, Ventnor, Isle of Wight **9**, 131
69 *Royal George Hotel, The*, Knutsford, Cheshire **2**, 132
70 *St George Hotel*, Darlington, County Durham **1**, 134
71 *Scole Inn, The*, Scole, Norfolk **7**, 136
72 *Shieldhill*, Biggar, Lanarkshire **14**, 137
73 *Ship Hotel, The*, Weybridge, Surrey **10**, 139
74 *Ston Easton Park*, Ston Easton, Somerset **8**, 141

- 75 *Stradley Park Hotel, The*, Llanelli, Dyfed **15**, 143
- 76 *Suffolk Hotel, The*, Bury St Edmunds, Suffolk **7**, 144
- 77 *Sunlaws House*, Kelso, Roxburghshrie **13**, 146
- 78 *Swan Hotel, The*, Knutsford, Cheshire **2**, 148
- 79 *Talbot Hotel, The*, Oundle, Northamptonshire **5**, 149
- 80 *Tibbie Shiels Inn*, St Mary's Loch, Selkirkshire **13**, 151
- 81 *Turnberry Hotel*, Turnberry, Ayrshire **14**, 153
- 82 *Tylney Hall*, Rotherwick, Hampshire **9**, 155
- 83 *Weston Manor Hotel*, Weston-on-the-Green, Oxfordshire **6**, 157
- 84 *White Horse Hotel, The*, Romsey, Hampshire **9**, 160

Regional Index of Hotels

Showing map nos. and page nos. for each hotel listed

NORTHUMBRIA MAP 1 (p163)
- [50] *Lord Crewe Arms, The*, Blanchland, County Durham, 95
- [51] *Lumley Castle*, Chester-le-Street, County Durham, 97
- [66] *Redworth Hall*, Redworth, County Durham, 127
- [70] *St George Hotel*, Darlington, County Durham, 134

NORTH WEST MAP 2 (p164)
- [29] *Dunkenhalgh Hotel*, Clayton-le-Moors, Lancashire, 57
- [78] *Swan Hotel, The*, Knutsford, Cheshire, 148
- [69] *Royal George Hotel, The*, Knutsford, Cheshire, 132

YORKSHIRE & HUMBERSIDE MAP 3 (p165)
- [10] *Black Swan Hotel, The*, Helmsley, Yorkshire, 18
- [23] *Crayke Castle*, Crayke, North Yorkshire, 46
- [24] *Crown Hotel and Posting House, The*, Bawtry, Yorkshire, 47
- [30] *Dweldapilton Hall Hotel*, Appleton-le-Moors, Yorkshire, 59
- [60] *Old Swan Hotel, The*, Harrogate, North Yorkshire, 116
- [64] *Ponden Hall*, Stanbury, West Yorkshire, 123

HEART OF ENGLAND MAP 4 (p166)
- [01] *Alveston Manor*, Stratford-upon-Avon, Warwickshire, 1
- [15] *Brownsover Hall*, Rugby, Warwickshire, 28
- [21] *Clearwell Castle*, Royal Forest of Dean, Gloucestershire, 41
- [27] *Dormy House Hotel*, Willersley Hill, Worcestershire, 53
- [33] *Ettington Park Hotel*, Alderminster, Warwickshire, 64
- [53] *Malt House, The*, Chipping Campden, Gloucestershire, 102
- [54] *Manor House Hotel, The*, Royal Leamington Spa, Warwickshire, 103
- [57] *New Hall*, Sutton Coldfield, Warwickshire, 109
- [65] *Prestbury House Hotel*, Prestbury, Gloucestershire, 125

EAST MIDLANDS MAP 5 (p167)
- [03] *Angel & Royal Hotel, The*, Grantham, Lincolnshire, 5
- [12] *Bosworth Hall*, Market Bosworth, Leicestershire, 22
- [41] *Grand Hotel, The*, Lincoln, Lincolnshire, 80

▫ *Lee Wood Hotel*, Buxton, Derbyshire, 92
▫ *Park International Hotel, The*, Leicester, Leicestershire, 120
▫ *Talbot Hotel, The*, Oundle, Northamptonshire, 149

THAMES & CHILTERNS MAP 6 (p168)
▫ *Berystede, The*, Sunninghill, Berkshire, 16
▫ *Weston Manor Hotel*, Weston-on-the-Green, Oxfordshire, 157

EAST ANGLIA MAP 7 (p169)
▫ *Bell Hotel, The*, Thetford, Norfolk, 14
▫ *Bull Hotel, The*, Peterborough, Cambridgeshire, 30
▫ *Bull Hotel, The*, Long Melford, Suffolk, 33
▫ *Duke's Head, The*, King's Lynn, Norfolk, 55
▫ *Golden Lion, The*, St Ives, Cambridgeshire, 78
▫ *Haycock Hotel, The*, Peterborough, Cambridgeshire, 83
▫ *Hintlesham Hall*, Hintlesham, Suffolk, 86
▫ *Knights Hill Hotel, The*, South Wootton, Norfolk, 88
▫ *Scole Inn, The*, Scole, Norfolk, 136
▫ *Suffolk Hotel, The*, Bury St Edmunds, Suffolk, 144

WEST COUNTRY MAP 8 (pp170-1)
▫ *Bedford Hotel, The*, Tavistock, Devon, 10
▫ *Beechfield House*, Melksham, Wiltshire, 12
▫ *Boringdon Hall*, Plympton, Devon, 20
▫ *Bradford Old Windmill*, Bradford-on-Avon, Wiltshire, 24
▫ *Burgh Island*, Bigbury-on-Sea, Devon, 35
▫ *Castle Hotel, The*, Taunton, Somerset, 39
▫ *Falmouth Hotel, The*, Falmouth, Cornwall, 66
▫ *Finnygook Inn, The*, Crafthole, Cornwall, 68
▫ *Forde Abbey*, Chard, Somerset, 70
▫ *Globe Hotel, The*, Topsham, Devon, 76
▫ *Leigh Park Hotel*, Bradford-on-Avon, Wiltshire, 94
▫ *Ston Easton Park*, Ston Easton, Somerset, 141

SOUTH OF ENGLAND MAP 9 (p172)
▫ *Dolphin Hotel, The*, Southampton, Hampshire, 52
▫ *Grosvenor Hotel, The*, Shaftesbury, Dorset, 82
▫ *Parkhill Hotel*, Lyndhurst, Hampshire, 122
▫ *Royal Hotel, The*, Ventnor, Isle of Wight, 131
▫ *Tylney Hall*, Rotherwick, Hampshire, 155
▫ *White Horse Hotel, The*, Romsey, Hampshire, 160

South East England Map 10 (p173)
- *Amberley Castle*, Amberley, West Sussex, 2
- *Brandshatch Place*, Fawkham, Kent, 26
- *Eastwell Manor*, Boughton Aluph, Kent, 61
- *Elvey Farm*, Pluckley, Kent, 62
- *George Hotel, The*, Crawley, Sussex, 74
- *Larkfield Priory Hotel*, Larkfield, Kent, 89
- *Lythe Hill Hotel*, Haslemere, Surrey, 99
- *Mermaid Hotel, The*, Rye, Sussex, 107
- *Ockenden Manor*, Cuckfield, Sussex, 111
- *Old Deanery, The*, Battle, East Sussex, 113
- *Regency Hotel, The*, Brighton, Sussex, 129
- *Ship Hotel, The*, Weybridge, Surrey, 139

Tayside & Grampian Map 11 (p174)
- *Atholl Palace*, Pitlochry, Perthshire, 6
- *Gairnshiel Lodge*, Ballater, Aberdeenshire, 72
- *Pannanich Wells Hotel*, Ballater, Royal Deeside, 118

Central Scotland Map 12 (p175)
- *Culcreuch Castle*, Fintry, Stirlingshire, 49
- *Learmonth Hotel, The*, Edinburgh, 91

Lowlands Map 13 (p176)
- *Comlongon Castle*, Clarencefield, Dumfries, 43
- *Marlfield House*, Kelso, Roxburghshire, 105
- *Sunlaws House*, Kelso, Roxburghshrie, 146
- *Tibbie Shiels Inn*, St Mary's Loch, Selkirkshire, 151

Strathclyde Map 14 (p177)
- *Shieldhill*, Biggar, Lanarkshire, 137
- *Turnberry Hotel*, Turnberry, Ayrshire, 153

Wales Map 15 (p178)
- *Castle Hotel, The*, Conwy, Gwynedd, 37
- *Stradley Park Hotel, The*, Llanelli, Dyfed, 143

Northern Ireland Map 16 (p179)
- *Ballygally Castle*, Ballygally, Co. Antrim, 8